Welcome to Learn German with Wordsearch Puzzles!

Inside this book, you will find 50 wordsearch puzzles each focusing on groups of German words to help you practice and improve your vocabulary. English translations are also included with each puzzle.

Words can be found inside the puzzle grid in straight lines running up, down, left, right or diagonally. Test your knowledge by drawing lines between the English and German word lists. Solutions are included in the back of this book for reference.

The last section includes a large number of review puzzles, which include some fill-in-the-blanks. Search for the translation in the puzzle grid. These review puzzles will help to reinforce your new vocabulary.

Note that only the capitalized words in the word lists are actually hidden inside the grid. One exception to this rule is for the German sharp S ("ß"), which only exists in lowercase form. The uppercase equivalent is a double capital 'SS'. In this book you will find "ß" in both the capitalized word lists and in the grid.

Good luck!

NUMBERS

01

When learning any language it is important to start with the basics. Here are some number translations to get started with.

V	D	R	E	I	Z	E	H	N	W	S	E	P	H	H
Ö	I	S	S	R	I	T	H	T	I	H	Z	N	N	H
P	T	E	E	U	W	E	A	E	M	I	G	E	I	V
F	T	V	R	O	Z	H	B	N	S	U	O	F	H	N
W	Ü	E	O	F	O	E	I	G	H	T	E	Ü	C	N
I	O	N	N	E	N	E	V	E	L	E	H	S	N	O
Ü	E	Ü	F	S	N	H	I	U	R	S	N	R	F	V
R	F	W	I	Z	W	Ö	L	F	U	D	N	O	E	I
U	T	X	Z	H	N	W	H	O	G	N	E	U	N	E
T	S	E	C	H	S	E	P	U	U	E	E	N	S	R
E	M	V	S	S	V	M	G	R	R	T	T	E	A	Z
M	A	I	U	L	A	O	E	T	T	I	F	H	S	E
S	C	F	E	I	N	E	F	E	N	N	I	A	C	H
A	H	W	L	E	T	T	L	E	O	M	F	W	H	N
N	T	H	I	R	T	E	E	N	D	E	E	N	P	E

ONE	EIN
TWO	ZWEI
THREE	DREI
FOUR	VIER
FIVE	FÜNF
SIX	SECHS
SEVEN	SIEBEN
EIGHT	ACHT
NINE	NEUN
TEN	ZEHN
ELEVEN	ELF
TWELVE	ZWÖLF
THIRTEEN	DREIZEHN
FOURTEEN	VIERZEHN
FIFTEEN	FÜNFZEHN

MORE NUMBERS

0 2

Whether you're looking for a particular address, or haggling for treasures at the market, here are some higher numbers to help you find what you're looking for.

E	N	A	S	I	N	E	E	T	N	E	V	E	S	H
I	N	H	E	Z	T	H	C	A	I	I	E	F	G	D
G	H	N	E	D	T	Y	S	Y	T	Y	I	I	I	E
H	E	S	I	Z	D	A	T	I	T	V	Z	H	Z	R
T	Z	C	A	O	N	R	U	N	E	B	C	E	T	D
E	H	S	N	H	O	U	E	S	E	B	N	N	H	N
E	C	O	E	F	U	V	E	I	E	W	Z	S	C	U
N	E	Ü	U	N	E	N	S	N	ß	N	T	E	A	H
E	S	E	N	S	A	V	D	E	E	I	D	C	H	E
E	G	I	Z	N	A	W	Z	E	S	N	G	H	E	N
T	R	H	I	M	E	N	T	T	R	E	Y	Z	E	O
Y	T	H	G	I	E	X	D	E	Y	T	R	I	H	T
V	I	E	R	Z	I	G	E	N	F	Y	T	G	U	T
Y	T	X	I	S	O	O	G	I	Z	F	N	Ü	F	L
T	R	E	D	N	U	H	F	N	Ü	F	Y	R	N	H

SIXTEEN
SEVENTEEN
EIGHTEEN
NINETEEN
TWENTY
THIRTY
FORTY
FIFTY
SIXTY
SEVENTY
EIGHTY
NINETY
ONE HUNDRED
FIVE hundred
THOUSAND

SECHZEHN
SIEBZEHN
ACHTZEHN
NEUNZEHN
ZWANZIG
DREIßIG
VIERZIG
FÜNFZIG
SECHZIG
SIEBZIG
ACHTZIG
NEUNZIG
HUNDERT
FÜNFHUNDERT
TAUSEND

DAYS OF THE WEEK

03

What day was the museum closed? When is that appointment? Here is a list of days to help keep your calendar in order.

S	D	G	T	W	O	C	H	E	N	E	N	D	E	L
E	E	I	A	T	O	D	A	Y	I	M	H	U	H	U
T	E	G	E	T	N	R	A	E	Y	I	S	C	N	D
T	N	U	T	N	N	D	R	E	S	T	L	M	O	T
S	T	T	H	E	S	N	S	O	A	T	I	W	E	W
A	U	F	U	V	N	T	O	G	M	W	E	E	K	H
N	E	R	R	S	E	D	A	S	S	O	S	R	E	Y
S	S	I	S	R	A	F	I	G	T	C	T	U	M	A
T	D	D	D	O	E	T	R	T	A	H	T	M	G	D
M	A	A	A	S	R	G	U	E	G	E	O	E	T	S
O	Y	Y	Y	L	Y	O	P	R	I	N	S	E	P	E
R	R	T	W	E	E	K	E	N	D	T	A	E	E	N
G	S	U	N	D	A	Y	F	A	E	A	A	H	R	D
E	M	O	N	T	A	G	Y	R	I	T	Y	G	R	E
N	P	A	R	D	O	N	N	E	R	S	T	A	G	W

MONDAY	MONTAG
TUESDAY	DIENSTAG
WEDNESDAY	MITTWOCH
THURSDAY	DONNERSTAG
FRIDAY	FREITAG
SATURDAY	SAMSTAG
SUNDAY	SONNTAG
WEEKEND	WOCHENENDE
TODAY	HEUTE
TOMORROW	MORGEN
YESTERDAY	GESTERN
WEEK	WOCHE
DAY	TAG

MONTHS

0 4

Speaking of calendars, do you have anything planned for next month? How about the month after that? Here is a list of months to study.

R	N	R	S	R	A	P	R	I	L	R	R	Y	F	A
E	D	O	E	U	R	E	I	E	E	D	E	E	R	Y
B	I	E	G	B	T	S	U	G	U	A	B	W	S	R
M	M	U	C	M	O	N	T	H	R	R	O	L	H	A
E	S	O	M	E	I	T	K	R	U	O	T	N	W	U
T	H	A	N	A	M	M	C	A	O	S	K	D	N	R
P	I	O	S	A	R	B	R	O	L	R	O	B	T	B
E	P	Y	Y	T	T	C	E	S	R	E	A	I	N	E
S	A	P	R	I	L	A	H	R	N	B	N	O	H	F
Z	F	D	T	A	J	L	O	R	T	M	V	D	C	T
H	R	C	T	U	U	E	N	O	V	E	M	B	E	R
U	I	Ä	L	A	L	N	D	R	M	Z	N	T	S	R
G	A	I	M	T	Y	D	A	B	M	E	J	U	N	I
J	A	N	U	A	R	A	E	J	T	D	O	P	J	A
M	N	T	J	A	H	R	E	B	M	E	T	P	E	S

JANUARY	JANUAR
FEBRUARY	FEBRUAR
MARCH	MÄRZ
APRIL	APRIL
MAY	MAI
JUNE	JUNI
JULY	JULI
AUGUST	AUGUST
SEPTEMBER	SEPTEMBER
OCTOBER	OKTOBER
NOVEMBER	NOVEMBER
DECEMBER	DEZEMBER
CALENDAR	KALENDER
MONTH	MONAT
YEAR	JAHR

TIME AND THE SEASONS

05

Be sure to memorize these "time" words, so you will always be on time. That is, at least until you finish inventing time travel. Keep up the hard work – you're almost there!

A	G	R	R	S	G	A	T	T	I	M	H	C	A	N
F	Y	D	Y	A	N	A	S	A	A	T	A	O	R	E
T	R	E	M	M	U	S	T	H	G	I	N	M	U	S
E	A	Ü	T	R	S	Y	U	E	M	E	I	S	O	R
R	N	T	H	C	A	N	N	M	I	N	U	T	E	L
N	E	A	T	L	V	K	D	K	U	T	N	F	M	R
O	J	T	A	R	I	T	E	T	G	N	I	R	P	S
O	E	M	N	R	E	N	E	E	O	L	M	E	I	E
N	V	O	O	I	A	M	G	N	W	L	H	T	D	M
A	E	R	M	H	W	H	M	S	E	C	O	N	D	O
C	N	G	C	T	E	U	O	O	O	I	U	I	N	R
S	I	E	Ü	R	T	B	N	W	S	K	N	W	E	N
R	N	N	B	U	H	S	T	E	E	D	E	I	B	I
N	G	S	A	P	G	E	H	S	A	Ü	E	E	A	N
M	T	O	E	I	H	H	H	Y	N	Y	C	E	T	G

WINTER	WINTER
SPRING	FRÜHLING
SUMMER	SOMMER
AUTUMN	HERBST
SECOND	SEKUNDE
MINUTE	MINUTE
HOUR	STUNDE
DAY	TAG
MONTH	MONAT
YEAR	JAHR
MORNING	MORGEN
AFTERNOON	NACHMITTAG
EVENING	ABEND
NIGHT	NACHT
WEEK	WOCHE

COLOURS

06

Modern televisions can display millions of different colours. Here is a list of just 13 for you to try to remember

```
S C H W A R Z O I A D N O P N
E O A P E Y G O T W S ß L E L
I U R D A B R A U N L T I O C
L A L N T A Ü U D I F W H E C
H L A B N Ü N E E L E L N A W
Y B O G I T F S T W F T O I O
M L E T I H W O A A L U Y O W
A E W T O R R S E L E E A C Z
G G O E I A O T S B R G R R Ü
E S L R N R E C E S R A G E G
N S L G B L A C K E O O E P G
T T E L O I V Y E F ß E W I C
A O Y I O F S N I D A P B N Y
T E V T E D E Y A O T E D K A
A T N E G A M E I V B E L ß N
```

BLACK	SCHWARZ
BLUE	BLAU
BROWN	BRAUN
CYAN	ZYAN
GRAY	GRAU
GREEN	GRÜN
MAGENTA	MAGENTA
ORANGE	ORANGE
PINK	ROSA
RED	ROT
VIOLET	VIOLETT
WHITE	WEIß
YELLOW	GELB

SHAPES

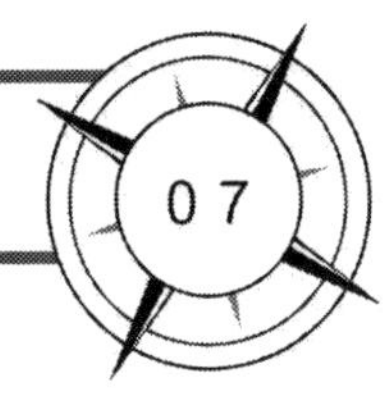

Here are some standard shapes, in both two and three dimensions.

P	E	L	E	G	U	K	K	C	E	S	H	C	E	S
R	E	D	P	R	I	H	H	L	H	R	N	F	D	I
E	E	N	H	Y	A	S	G	E	E	H	E	L	I	X
C	P	D	T	L	R	N	X	D	L	A	V	O	M	M
T	S	K	N	A	A	A	N	H	U	I	O	V	A	L
A	I	C	D	I	G	I	M	G	L	C	X	T	R	L
N	E	E	R	O	L	O	H	I	I	E	A	H	Y	F
G	R	T	N	Y	C	Y	N	R	D	R	G	N	P	R
L	K	H	Z	U	E	T	C	W	D	E	F	E	C	K
E	C	C	U	B	E	L	A	A	S	H	I	Y	K	A
F	E	E	E	N	E	E	U	G	E	P	T	Ü	T	A
R	I	R	R	T	N	Q	R	V	O	S	C	P	U	M
Ü	E	H	H	O	H	T	S	H	S	N	E	A	D	R
W	R	O	C	L	K	C	E	F	N	Ü	F	M	U	Y
U	D	N	C	S	Q	U	A	R	E	P	R	N	Ü	Ü

CIRCLE
CONE
CUBE
CYLINDER
HELIX
HEXAGON
OCTAGON
OVAL
PENTAGON
PYRAMID
RECTANGLE
SPHERE
SQUARE
TRIANGLE

KREIS
KEGEL
WÜRFEL
ZYLINDER
HELIX
SECHSECK
ACHTECK
OVAL
FÜNFECK
PYRAMIDE
RECHTECK
KUGEL
QUADRAT
DREIECK

THE BODY

08

The human body is a remarkable thing, with hundreds of specialized parts that we take for granted every day. Here is a list of some important parts of the body to remember.

E	I	D	H	O	Z	E	H	T	R	N	E	S	U	D
L	M	N	K	A	N	A	O	R	L	A	D	M	A	H
H	O	I	N	O	N	A	E	O	H	M	O	Ä	I	Ü
Ö	I	E	E	N	P	E	E	T	R	P	S	N	W	F
H	U	B	L	E	T	F	U	A	M	R	A	L	I	T
L	A	F	E	P	E	O	G	R	E	L	E	W	M	E
E	L	N	G	E	M	Ö	N	M	D	G	A	U	N	I
S	S	I	D	H	H	E	O	P	D	I	N	P	T	D
H	L	I	N	F	E	A	T	I	S	D	E	U	S	E
C	A	S	A	R	L	A	O	T	S	I	R	W	Z	S
A	I	A	H	S	I	Ä	E	F	Ä	L	H	C	S	T
I	A	D	M	L	R	A	C	L	P	T	F	T	R	O
S	C	A	L	F	S	Ö	H	H	E	E	L	A	B	O
F	O	E	S	R	E	F	E	E	E	D	A	W	Ü	O
E	I	H	D	D	E	A	H	G	I	H	I	P	I	H

ARM	ARM
ARMPIT	ACHSELHÖHLE
CALF	WADE
HAIR	HAAR
HEAD	KOPF
HEEL	FERSE
HIP	HÜFTE
LEG	BEIN
MOUTH	MUND
PALM	HANDFLÄCHE
TEMPLE	SCHLÄFE
TOE	ZEH
TONGUE	ZUNGE
WAIST	TAILLE
WRIST	HANDGELENK

THE BODY - PART 2

09

Here is a list of some more equally important body parts for you to let sink into your head.

B	R	U	S	T	Ä	F	U	ß	C	S	H	R	R	O
R	D	I	H	O	T	F	I	N	G	E	R	A	W	I
U	B	E	D	A	U	M	E	N	F	E	F	D	T	P
S	M	A	L	Z	N	G	T	E	G	I	S	T	P	O
T	U	T	D	P	O	D	E	U	N	E	A	Ä	W	T
W	H	O	S	B	P	O	A	L	U	L	R	T	ß	T
A	T	C	L	A	W	I	E	R	B	B	G	O	T	S
R	R	L	I	S	E	D	N	R	U	O	C	I	T	H
Z	E	R	T	S	O	R	E	N	T	W	H	I	L	O
E	E	N	O	R	E	T	B	E	T	R	R	A	R	U
P	R	O	O	L	L	G	A	Y	O	N	O	N	N	L
G	D	S	F	U	N	A	S	E	C	A	F	H	E	D
D	A	E	H	E	R	O	F	T	K	O	E	M	H	E
R	P	C	N	S	ß	A	S	C	H	U	L	T	E	R
E	S	H	O	U	L	D	E	R	B	L	A	D	E	S

BREAST	BRUST
BUTTOCK	GESÄß
EAR	OHR
ELBOW	ELLBOGEN
EYE	AUGE
FACE	GESICHT
FINGER	FINGER
FOOT	FUß
FOREHEAD	STIRN
HAND	HAND
NIPPLE	BRUSTWARZE
NOSE	NASE
SHOULDER	SCHULTER
SHOULDER BLADE	SCHULTERBLATT
THUMB	DAUMEN

THE BODY - PART 3

10

Let's face it, the body is a complicated thing.
Here is a final list of things that are attached to you.

L	E	G	A	N	R	E	G	N	I	F	E	U	M	V
O	T	L	I	E	S	N	E	C	K	R	S	R	R	A
B	E	H	E	K	N	K	A	E	N	E	A	A	A	K
E	C	O	F	H	C	Y	Ä	O	I	R	E	F	E	Ä
R	Y	H	T	Ü	C	A	E	H	E	T	N	P	R	C
S	L	U	R	L	T	Ö	B	T	G	N	Z	Ä	O	S
C	A	E	E	N	K	O	N	O	I	I	Ä	T	F	U
H	E	B	V	H	T	U	N	K	D	Y	H	Ö	Ü	K
E	A	S	A	A	E	E	A	I	H	Y	N	T	N	G
N	L	L	O	A	N	A	T	P	K	C	E	I	L	R
K	S	K	W	A	N	G	E	Ö	N	S	O	U	E	Ä
E	T	O	N	N	G	N	R	A	C	H	E	E	K	R
L	A	P	H	A	N	P	M	U	S	C	L	E	S	I
A	Ä	C	O	T	E	E	T	H	D	I	O	N	U	O
L	I	A	N	R	E	G	N	I	F	Ä	Y	E	M	F

ANKLE	KNÖCHEL
BACK	RÜCKEN
BODY	KÖRPER
CHEEK	WANGE
CHIN	KINN
FINGERNAIL	FINGERNAGEL
FOREARM	UNTERARM
KNEE	KNIE
MUSCLES	MUSKELN
NAVEL	NABEL
NECK	HALS
SKIN	HAUT
TEETH	ZÄHNE
THIGH	OBERSCHENKEL

INSIDE THE BODY

11

Just when you thought you had escaped the anatomy lesson, we thought that we should mention a few of the hidden squishy things that keep our bodies running smoothly

S	A	N	H	U	D	E	N	N	M	U	T	C	E	R
R	E	B	E	L	D	E	B	L	O	O	D	N	G	R
M	E	N	G	I	G	Ü	T	G	E	H	I	R	N	N
E	R	W	I	A	R	Z	N	S	B	T	C	O	U	E
T	T	A	M	T	T	E	R	N	S	N	K	H	L	N
T	E	N	D	U	S	I	T	E	D	B	D	Ü	I	E
S	S	M	N	T	E	E	T	R	H	A	A	A	A	V
H	T	N	H	I	S	N	T	A	A	A	R	P	A	L
E	I	E	I	R	I	A	T	N	R	B	M	M	I	F
A	L	D	H	E	N	A	M	T	I	A	I	V	R	N
R	F	R	G	P	V	S	E	S	P	L	E	E	N	I
T	T	R	H	A	E	R	P	R	Z	R	L	A	L	E
U	A	T	B	E	I	H	H	A	A	N	H	A	E	R
L	U	N	G	E	H	C	A	M	O	T	S	R	M	E
B	P	F	S	Y	E	N	D	I	K	C	H	M	L	S

ARTERIES	ARTERIEN
BLOOD	BLUT
BRAIN	GEHIRN
HEART	HERZ
KIDNEY	NIERE
LARGE INTESTINE	DICKDARM
LIVER	LEBER
LUNG	LUNGE
RECTUM	MASTDARM
SMALL INTESTINE	DÜNNDARM
SPLEEN	MILZ
STOMACH	MAGEN
VEINS	VENEN

LAND AND SEA

12

The world is a big place. Approximately 70% of the Earth's surface area is covered by water. Here is a list of some of the world's continents, oceans and seas.

A	K	I	R	E	M	A	D	R	O	N	T	E	N	Q
N	B	I	O	E	P	O	R	U	E	S	C	A	O	K
A	A	T	T	O	F	Ü	T	R	U	Ü	I	N	A	C
E	H	F	R	N	S	B	E	R	E	D	F	A	A	A
N	A	U	R	E	A	H	O	R	N	A	I	N	N	L
A	E	T	T	I	C	L	M	I	R	M	C	T	O	B
R	C	O	L	S	K	S	T	E	A	E	A	A	Z	Ü
R	R	I	I	A	H	A	E	A	Y	R	P	R	E	I
E	T	D	R	T	N	M	M	Z	C	I	C	K	A	T
T	N	B	U	F	L	T	G	T	R	K	S	T	N	O
I	L	O	C	E	A	N	I	A	H	A	O	I	I	A
D	S	H	T	I	R	C	H	C	I	T	W	S	E	C
E	I	T	S	P	A	Z	I	F	I	K	R	H	N	S
M	I	A	U	R	E	W	A	G	D	G	I	O	C	T
M	R	E	E	M	R	A	L	O	P	D	R	O	N	S

NORTH america
SOUTH america
EUROPE
ASIA
AFRICA
OCEANIA
ANTARCTICA
PACIFIC ocean
ATLANTIC ocean
INDIAN ocean
ARCTIC ocean
MEDITERRANEAN sea
BLACK sea
RED sea

NORDAMERIKA
SÜDAMERIKA
EUROPA
ASIEN
AFRIKA
OZEANIEN
ANTARKTIS
PAZIFIK
ATLANTIK
INDISCHER ozean
NORDPOLARMEER
MITTELMEER
SCHWARZES meer
ROTES meer

MAP OF THE WORLD

13

There is much more to the world than continents and oceans. Here are some other interesting features that you might find on a world map.

```
G E B I R G S K E T T E Ü Q O
L Z U G T E D P P N F L U ß A
A L N O H N E M R Y L E W T L
N A D I A O D M R O H S O E U
D I E L V N D T P A V N A L S
W E S W A O N N L S I I A S N
M I S R E U R B A E S K N L I
S E T E O I I P T E E B A C N
S S A C R N Y L E I C T A R E
T D A T S T P U A H I O I S P
A H T E I S N E U P A V T M A
T H L C I E P L A T E A U Ü O
E M E N B E A C H R D S R E T
E O Z E A N W Ü S T E T R ß O
L E G N A R N I A T N U O M A
```

BEACH	STRAND
CAPITAL	HAUPTSTADT
CITY	STADT
COUNTRY	LAND
DESERT	WÜSTE
ISLAND	INSEL
LAKE	SEE
MOUNTAIN RANGE	GEBIRGSKETTE
OCEAN	OZEAN
PENINSULA	HALBINSEL
PLATEAU	PLATEAU
PROVINCE	PROVINZ
RIVER	FLUß
SEA	MEER
STATE	BUNDESSTAAT

CITY MAP

14

A good map can help you figure out where you want to go, or help you figure out where the heck you actually are. Here is a list of a few things that you might find on a map.

D	A	O	R	L	I	A	R	E	T	R	O	R	O	V
R	B	A	I	P	D	S	A	S	Y	E	E	S	U	E
A	R	N	K	A	T	R	T	R	U	V	L	B	L	N
V	I	D	R	R	U	R	A	A	T	I	T	R	O	I
E	D	E	A	K	E	T	B	V	D	R	B	Ü	L	L
L	G	ß	P	E	E	E	O	A	E	T	N	C	B	D
U	E	ß	T	M	T	S	L	B	H	L	T	K	C	A
O	H	H	E	D	B	T	B	H	A	N	U	E	H	O
B	T	C	I	R	T	S	I	D	E	H	H	O	I	R
A	V	T	U	I	E	G	L	M	ß	T	N	O	B	L
N	I	B	Y	U	H	U	U	U	E	H	J	N	F	I
R	U	V	N	W	G	N	L	A	M	K	N	E	D	A
S	I	E	A	D	O	F	O	H	D	E	I	R	F	R
E	V	Y	N	M	A	N	R	T	H	X	A	E	E	Ü
A	L	L	E	E	H	E	I	S	E	N	B	A	H	N

AVENUE	ALLEE
BOULEVARD	BOULEVARD
BRIDGE	BRÜCKE
CEMETARY	FRIEDHOF
DISTRICT	STADTTEIL
HIGHWAY	AUTOBAHN
MONUMENT	DENKMAL
PARK	PARK
RAILROAD LINE	EISENBAHN
RAILROAD station	BAHNHOF
RIVER	FLUß
STREET	STRAßE
SUBURBS	VORORTE

WEATHER

15

No matter how well you plan things, you simply can't control the weather. Here are some weather terms that might either make your day, or ruin it.

G	E	F	R	I	E	R	E	N	D	E	R	N	R	C
A	N	G	T	R	A	F	W	O	B	N	I	A	R	I
S	H	L	N	O	M	R	A	W	L	A	I	O	L	R
T	T	L	D	I	E	O	Y	U	R	L	E	A	G	T
S	T	A	B	L	N	S	F	Y	B	N	F	N	R	E
P	W	U	R	S	E	T	V	Ö	A	N	I	D	D	M
R	W	Q	D	K	D	A	H	C	E	Z	E	R	N	O
Ü	T	S	O	R	E	U	I	G	E	T	R	I	I	R
H	A	S	U	H	R	R	O	E	I	I	U	Z	W	A
R	I	C	N	R	R	B	R	L	E	L	A	Z	O	B
E	K	H	I	U	N	F	V	E	C	B	R	L	L	G
G	R	K	H	E	D	N	N	E	G	E	R	E	K	R
E	A	U	G	I	R	U	T	A	R	E	P	M	E	T
N	S	E	M	R	A	W	I	I	W	I	N	D	N	R
E	R	U	T	A	R	E	P	M	E	T	T	S	I	M

BAROMETRIC pressure — LUFTDRUCK
CLOUDS — WOLKEN
DRIZZLE — SPRÜHREGEN
FREEZING rain — GEFRIERENDER regen
FROST — RAUREIF
HEAVY RAIN — STARKER REGEN
HURRICANE — HURRIKAN
LIGHTNING — BLITZ
MIST — DUNST
RAIN — REGEN
RAINBOW — REGENBOGEN
SQUALL — BÖ
TEMPERATURE — TEMPERATUR
WARM — WARM
WIND — WIND

MORE WEATHER

16

Today's forecast says that you have a 99% chance of learning some important weather terms. Here are some additional weather related words.

```
S T R O P I C A L S T O R M M
L L N T E E A A I W E D C T R
E N E H N U F I A T E Y U L U
I A E E O H I S H D C O E G T
C L A G T D S M A L P G W O S
H D L V E E A T O S A O I H R
T D S I R R H N R H D F R D E
E U N H G S E E R A T H B N H
R N O L C H T E N O E R E U C
R S W H E A T R N T T N L A S
E T N P W B O R H H K S S T I
G E W I T T E R A A C R T S P
E I C O L D D N L I Z S U A O
N O O H P Y T T E B N E R N R
E T H U N D E R S T O R M O T
```

COLD	KALT
CYCLONE	WIRBELSTURM
DEW	TAU
FOG	NEBEL
HAIL	HAGEL
HAZE	DUNST
LIGHT RAIN	LEICHTER REGEN
SLEET	SCHNEEREGEN
SNOW	SCHNEE
THUNDERSTORM	GEWITTER
TORNADO	TORNADO
TROPICAL STORM	TROPISCHER STURM
TYPHOON	TAIFUN
WATERSPOUT	WASSERHOSE

ANIMAL KINGDOM

17

There are many wild and wonderful creatures out there. Why don't you take a few minutes to familiarize yourself with a few of them?

B	G	R	O	U	N	D	H	O	G	H	A	S	E	T
A	E	M	T	O	C	A	M	E	L	P	U	S	S	N
C	R	S	R	A	U	G	A	J	U	E	C	N	E	I
K	S	U	E	J	A	G	U	A	R	H	L	A	D	E
E	R	K	M	L	N	X	L	N	W	H	L	R	E	W
N	L	A	R	E	P	O	T	E	D	O	A	A	F	H
H	S	M	B	S	L	F	I	W	P	R	M	I	Y	C
Ö	A	E	Y	A	E	N	E	O	I	S	A	G	E	S
R	O	L	M	E	R	T	R	R	Y	E	O	E	T	L
N	M	A	E	W	K	C	Y	B	D	D	S	F	G	E
C	H	I	P	M	U	N	K	G	U	E	U	E	H	H
H	M	G	I	P	U	E	O	M	D	C	T	A	L	C
E	L	P	I	N	E	R	U	D	H	H	R	R	E	A
N	P	N	O	T	O	L	E	S	S	E	O	R	H	T
R	E	I	T	L	E	M	R	U	M	D	L	A	W	S

CAMEL	KAMEL
CHIPMUNK	BACKENHÖRNCHEN
DOG	HUND
DONKEY	ESEL
FOX	FUCHS
GROUNDHOG	WALDMURMELTIER
HARE	HASE
HORSE	PFERD
JAGUAR	JAGUAR
LEMUR	LEMURE
LLAMA	LAMA
MULE	MAULTIER
PIG	SCHWEIN
PORCUPINE	STACHELSCHWEIN
WEASEL	WIESEL

ANIMAL KINGDOM 2

18

The diversity of life on this planet is truly astounding. Animals have found ways to survive in the toughest of climates and conditions. The least you can do is try to remember some of their names.

N	N	E	H	C	N	I	N	A	K	E	S	O	O	M
I	I	O	O	O	H	T	E	G	E	P	A	R	D	H
E	N	R	O	H	S	A	N	H	E	Ä	R	H	H	E
W	W	L	C	C	E	W	A	S	C	H	B	Ä	R	D
H	I	L	E	S	C	M	T	M	E	I	A	N	I	G
C	E	L	I	F	S	A	N	E	S	H	C	O	E	E
S	A	G	D	T	F	O	R	E	I	T	N	E	R	H
D	E	R	E	B	S	Ü	D	T	E	B	A	E	O	O
L	B	R	I	I	O	R	B	R	H	H	I	R	L	G
I	U	A	B	B	A	A	T	A	A	W	V	S	E	C
W	F	U	B	P	O	I	R	T	M	S	A	P	O	X
W	F	O	O	O	B	U	E	E	S	N	P	U	P	N
U	A	E	U	B	O	E	W	O	T	O	G	M	A	N
H	L	I	A	O	H	N	W	Ü	E	A	O	A	R	O
S	O	R	E	C	O	N	I	H	R	T	H	R	D	N

BABOON	PAVIAN
BISON	BISON
BUFFALO	BÜFFEL
CARIBOU	RENTIER
CHEETAH	GEPARD
COUGAR	PUMA
HAMSTER	HAMSTER
HEDGEHOG	IGEL
LEOPARD	LEOPARD
MOOSE	ELCH
OX	OCHSE
RABBIT	KANINCHEN
RACCOON	WASCHBÄR
RHINOCEROS	NASHORN
WILD BOAR	WILDSCHWEIN

ANIMAL KINGDOM 3

19

New species are being found every year in caves, rainforests and oceans. Maybe you can find one and name it after yourself. Here are some more animals to study.

A	G	O	R	I	L	L	A	O	P	O	S	S	U	M
K	N	A	G	B	E	N	I	U	R	U	G	N	Ä	K
N	D	A	A	I	T	S	I	I	M	L	I	V	E	D
U	W	T	T	I	R	T	N	A	R	A	T	T	E	C
K	W	A	L	U	N	A	T	U	G	N	A	R	O	Y
S	E	O	L	A	G	O	F	I	R	F	E	M	Ä	S
W	P	E	F	L	P	N	R	F	L	A	O	N	T	C
E	A	E	Z	O	A	A	A	E	E	O	T	I	E	H
L	L	L	P	N	F	B	D	R	R	T	N	L	P	I
E	L	P	L	F	A	E	Y	A	O	K	T	P	O	M
P	I	L	E	A	R	P	G	H	T	L	E	F	L	P
H	R	A	I	M	B	N	M	I	N	Ö	U	E	E	A
A	O	U	A	O	A	Y	E	I	O	W	F	R	T	N
N	G	U	R	K	N	R	B	N	H	E	E	D	N	S
T	S	O	P	O	S	S	U	M	O	C	L	B	A	E

ANTELOPE	ANTILOPE
BAT	FLEDERMAUS
CHIMPANZEE	SCHIMPANSE
ELEPHANT	ELEFANT
GIRAFFE	GIRAFFE
GORILLA	GORILLA
HIPPOPOTAMUS	NILPFERD
KANGAROO	KÄNGURU
LION	LÖWE
OPOSSUM	OPOSSUM
ORANGUTAN	ORANG-UTAN
RAT	RATTE
SKUNK	STINKTIER
tasmanian DEVIL	tasmanischer TEUFEL
WALLABY	WALLABY

ANIMAL KINGDOM 4

20

The animal kingdom is a huge place, and so far we've only covered animals that have their feet firmly planted on the ground. So before we take to the air and to the sea, here is a final list of land creatures

N	E	H	C	N	I	E	W	H	C	S	R	E	E	M
E	B	N	G	O	A	T	L	B	C	U	E	N	I	M
C	O	I	S	I	T	H	L	H	D	A	V	Ä	O	N
T	A	L	B	I	P	A	W	S	A	M	A	Y	T	E
W	Z	T	G	E	C	A	W	O	C	R	E	H	U	H
N	N	E	Ö	K	R	N	E	I	H	H	B	T	S	C
H	R	G	B	Z	T	E	Ä	N	S	M	A	E	O	N
B	O	E	B	R	R	Y	P	H	I	O	E	F	Z	R
S	A	Ä	R	Ä	A	H	E	E	D	U	N	N	E	Ö
R	R	D	B	Z	I	E	G	E	H	S	G	G	A	H
A	T	S	G	H	P	K	A	T	Z	E	I	I	U	H
H	I	B	F	E	I	E	W	H	O	T	N	K	O	C
E	R	M	L	E	R	O	A	H	P	S	U	C	O	I
T	G	E	O	C	L	E	R	R	I	U	Q	S	D	E
A	M	E	W	F	V	P	O	L	A	R	B	E	A	R

BADGER	DACHS
BEAVER	BIBER
BLACK BEAR	SCHWARZBÄR
CAT	KATZE
COW	KUH
MOUSE	MAUS
GOAT	ZIEGE
GUINEA PIG	MEERSCHWEINCHEN
HYENA	HYÄNE
POLAR BEAR	EISBÄR
SHEEP	SCHAF
SQUIRREL	EICHHÖRNCHEN
TIGER	TIGER
WOLF	WOLF
ZEBRA	ZEBRA

BIRDS

21

There are thousands of different species of birds, some of which are actually flightless. Here are a few that you might see circling high above, or waddling around your feet

D	R	E	K	C	E	P	D	O	O	W	E	U	L	E
R	R	F	N	D	N	R	A	D	L	E	R	P	I	A
I	A	S	L	N	U	ß	A	W	D	O	I	O	T	L
B	V	H	N	A	U	C	O	B	N	G	S	F	G	B
G	E	E	A	A	M	B	K	I	E	T	T	O	I	A
N	N	P	R	K	G	I	U	O	R	E	B	U	A	T
I	E	T	E	L	O	G	N	I	M	A	L	F	G	R
M	S	R	O	N	N	L	C	G	P	O	F	E	S	O
M	E	U	U	I	G	H	I	E	O	S	I	L	T	S
U	G	T	P	T	E	U	L	B	A	E	G	G	U	L
H	O	H	N	A	L	I	I	T	R	T	T	A	R	T
R	O	A	M	E	K	U	N	N	I	I	Y	E	K	A
T	S	H	M	A	N	T	V	N	A	C	I	L	E	P
L	E	N	N	I	E	I	M	N	C	T	W	I	Y	ß
H	A	L	B	A	T	R	O	S	S	P	E	C	H	T

ALBATROSS	ALBATROS
DUCK	ENTE
EAGLE	ADLER
FLAMINGO	FLAMINGO
GOOSE	GANS
HUMMINGBIRD	KOLIBRI
OSTRICH	STRAUß
OWL	EULE
PELICAN	PELIKAN
PENGUIN	PINGUIN
PIGEON	TAUBE
RAVEN	RABE
TURKEY	TRUTHAHN
VULTURE	GEIER
WOODPECKER	SPECHT

UNDER THE SEA

22

The Earth's oceans and lakes might look calm on the surface, but below they are teeming with life. Here are a few creatures you might find frolicking just beneath the surface

E W Ö L E E S E A U R C H I N
E N T N A R W A L E G I E E S
B D H S I F L A O S E O S H H
R E M M U H W A U T D H A C S
E L L I Ö ß P R E T T R S T T
C P A U I L L L Ü S K I I S A
P H B E G A O M O N F N U E R
O I W N W A M B R D T P ß E F
R N N O I L A E S E O H O H I
P A F K E A T ß N T R N R U S
O R W R Ö S I F C O E D L N H
I W O H E T I O R R E R A D N
S H A E A S C H W E R T W A L
E A S L C L E R A N O T Y C S
E L A H W R E L L I K Ü S A T

BELUGA	WEIßWAL
DOLPHIN	DELPHIN
FISH	FISCH
KILLER WHALE	SCHWERTWAL
LOBSTER	HUMMER
NARWHAL	NARWAL
OCTOPUS	TINTENFISCH
PORPOISE	TÜMMLER
SEA LION	SEELÖWE
SEA URCHIN	SEEIGEL
SEAL	SEEHUND
SHARK	HAI
STARFISH	SEESTERN
WALRUS	WALROß
WHALE	WAL

INSECTS

23

Insects may be annoying when they're buzzing around your ears, or trying to suck your blood, but they are a crucial part of the food chain. Here's a list of a few insects to squash off your vocabulary list

Y	G	N	I	L	R	E	T	T	E	M	H	C	S	E
Y	L	F	E	S	R	O	H	Z	I	K	A	D	E	N
E	L	F	N	F	L	I	E	G	E	T	E	B	O	E
L	P	F	R	B	R	E	M	S	E	H	E	T	P	I
L	H	O	N	E	Y	B	E	E	S	L	S	S	E	B
O	R	F	F	O	T	V	H	T	B	I	E	T	I	G
W	U	L	L	T	G	T	N	M	I	W	N	P	N	I
J	E	O	E	I	U	A	U	A	E	M	O	R	R	N
A	D	H	M	K	B	B	R	B	T	T	R	N	O	O
C	O	E	M	S	Y	E	A	D	I	E	O	E	E	H
K	V	I	U	O	D	D	L	U	M	B	N	C	T	F
E	Y	A	H	M	A	H	Q	L	R	S	M	R	N	A
T	L	O	R	C	L	S	A	M	E	I	S	E	O	K
L	F	S	I	L	O	U	S	E	T	S	G	L	Ä	H
Y	S	C	S	M	A	R	I	E	N	K	Ä	F	E	R

ANT	AMEISE
BUMBLEBEE	HUMMEL
BUTTERFLY	SCHMETTERLING
CICADA	ZIKADE
DRAGONFLY	LIBELLE
FLEA	FLOH
FLY	FLIEGE
HONEYBEE	HONIGBIENE
HORNET	HORNISSE
HORSEFLY	BREMSE
LADYBUG	MARIENKÄFER
LOUSE	LAUS
MOSQUITO	MOSKITO
TERMITE	TERMITE
YELLOWJACKET	WESPE

REPTILES & AMPHIBIANS

24

We can't leave the animal kingdom without first paying some respect to our reptile and amphibian friends. That would be cold blooded of us.

E	D	R	A	Z	I	L	R	O	T	I	N	O	M	I
G	F	W	A	R	A	N	K	N	O	H	T	Y	P	R
N	E	R	N	S	A	T	I	R	E	P	I	V	A	E
A	N	W	O	U	C	R	O	C	O	D	I	L	E	D
L	O	O	G	S	O	H	D	O	A	K	L	T	H	N
H	E	E	E	A	C	A	I	L	R	I	O	R	D	A
C	L	K	L	L	E	H	L	L	G	A	E	D	E	M
S	Ä	A	T	A	E	I	L	A	D	U	H	S	I	A
R	M	N	R	M	G	M	T	A	T	K	H	E	N	L
E	A	S	U	A	O	O	A	V	N	C	R	L	O	A
P	H	Y	T	N	R	S	I	H	E	G	T	Ö	H	S
P	C	O	M	D	F	P	U	D	C	N	E	E	T	I
A	R	R	C	E	E	N	I	G	U	A	N	A	Y	E
L	I	Z	A	R	D	E	T	Ö	R	K	O	T	P	B
K	R	A	T	T	L	E	S	N	A	K	E	E	E	T

ALLIGATOR	ALLIGATOR
CHAMELEON	CHAMÄLEON
CROCODILE	KROKODIL
FROG	FROSCH
IGUANA	LEGUAN
LIZARD	EIDECHSE
MONITOR LIZARD	WARAN
PYTHON	PYTHON
RATTLESNAKE	KLAPPERSCHLANGE
SALAMANDER	SALAMANDER
SNAKE	SCHLANGE
TOAD	KRÖTE
TURTLE	SCHILDKRÖTE
VIPER	VIPER

LIFE

25

Finally, we have a category for reviewing some different categories of life. You may be familiar with many of these by now.

F	S	E	R	E	I	T	L	E	T	U	E	B	B	R
L	T	R	O	D	E	N	T	S	M	L	X	N	I	E
E	C	A	L	G	E	N	L	A	C	B	O	E	R	S
I	E	I	S	H	R	A	R	A	C	H	N	I	D	S
S	S	S	C	Ä	M	S	R	R	N	N	E	B	S	E
C	N	S	U	M	U	N	S	N	A	H	I	I	N	R
H	I	A	A	P	I	G	A	G	E	N	L	H	E	F
F	D	M	I	V	A	H	E	R	S	N	I	P	T	N
R	Ä	A	O	B	C	T	B	T	E	R	T	M	A	E
E	L	R	R	T	I	I	A	T	I	I	P	A	M	Z
S	E	U	T	E	V	H	K	L	L	E	E	P	I	N
S	G	R	R	O	S	E	P	E	G	R	R	H	R	A
E	Ö	E	R	I	S	D	S	M	F	A	A	E	P	L
R	V	E	F	N	P	R	I	M	A	T	E	S	E	F
V	S	P	I	N	N	E	N	T	I	E	R	E	L	P

ALGAE	ALGEN
AMPHIBIANS	AMPHIBIEN
ARACHNIDS	SPINNENTIERE
BIRDS	VÖGEL
CARNIVORES	FLEISCHFRESSER
FISH	FISCHE
HERBIVORES	PFLANZENFRESSER
INSECTS	INSEKTEN
MAMMALS	SÄUGETIERE
MARSUPIALS	BEUTELTIERE
PRIMATES	PRIMATEN
REPTILES	REPTILIEN
RODENTS	NAGETIERE

FAMILY

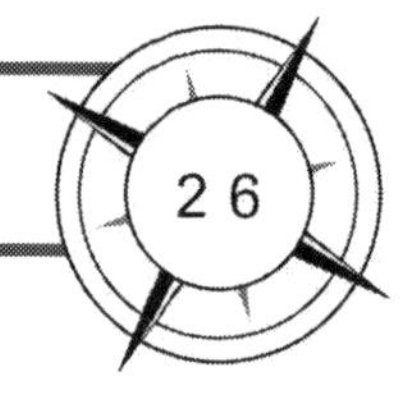

Are you married?
Do you have any siblings?
Here is a list of terms that will help you
to describe your nearest and dearest.

R	R	E	T	T	U	M	ß	O	R	G	O	S	N	Y
E	E	E	S	R	L	C	E	E	W	M	H	R	E	S
H	T	H	D	O	C	H	I	L	D	R	E	N	C	V
T	H	S	T	N	H	L	M	U	B	T	M	H	A	N
O	C	A	N	A	I	N	H	R	L	O	W	T	I	D
M	O	N	U	M	F	K	U	E	T	E	E	C	S	T
D	T	P	A	S	D	D	T	H	S	R	H	P	O	G
N	O	F	A	S	E	C	E	T	E	T	P	E	N	R
A	E	A	H	R	C	R	E	B	E	T	E	E	K	O
R	S	M	C	E	E	R	E	C	R	N	N	L	E	ß
G	I	I	D	G	I	N	N	T	U	O	E	A	L	V
F	S	L	R	E	N	O	T	R	T	N	T	F	T	A
O	T	Y	I	I	S	I	L	S	D	U	C	H	F	T
R	E	T	H	G	U	A	D	H	E	D	M	L	E	E
I	R	W	E	G	R	A	N	D	F	A	T	H	E	R

AUNT	TANTE
BROTHER	BRUDER
CHILDREN	KINDER
DAUGHTER	TOCHTER
FAMILY	FAMILIE
FATHER	VATER
GRANDFATHER	GROßVATER
GRANDMOTHER	GROßMUTTER
MOTHER	MUTTER
NEPHEW	NEFFE
NIECE	NICHTE
PARENTS	ELTERN
SISTER	SCHWESTER
SON	SOHN
UNCLE	ONKEL

FAMILY - EXTENDED

27

Here are some more family members that you might be particularly fond of (or perhaps not).

R	S	C	H	W	I	E	G	E	R	V	A	T	E	R
E	E	R	U	R	G	R	O	ß	E	L	T	E	R	N
T	U	T	A	R	E	R	E	T	S	I	S	E	U	S
T	R	E	H	A	G	R	A	C	O	C	F	C	E	T
U	G	E	T	G	E	R	H	N	H	S	R	N	D	N
M	R	S	H	T	U	W	O	W	D	O	A	L	N	E
R	O	N	T	T	A	A	Ä	ß	I	S	U	E	A	R
E	ß	E	E	G	O	G	D	N	M	F	O	K	R	A
G	V	S	E	R	E	M	N	D	A	U	E	N	G	P
E	A	R	H	R	D	A	F	I	N	D	T	E	T	D
I	T	E	I	N	M	L	H	E	L	A	S	T	A	N
W	E	N	K	E	L	K	I	N	D	E	R	Q	E	A
H	R	E	H	T	O	R	B	H	S	Ä	K	G	R	R
C	S	E	H	N	I	S	U	O	C	T	A	N	G	G
S	D	N	A	B	S	U	H	T	F	A	T	H	E	R

BROTHER-in-law	SCHWAGER
COUSIN	VETTER
FATHER-in-law	SCHWIEGERVATER
grandCHILDREN	ENKELKINDER
GRANDDAUGHTER	ENKELIN
GRANDSON	ENKEL
GREAT grandfather	URGROßVATER
GREAT GRANDmother	URGROßMUTTER
great GRANDPARENTS	URGROßELTERN
HUSBAND	EHEMANN
MOTHER-in-law	SCHWIEGERMUTTER
SISTER-in-law	SCHWÄGERIN
WIFE	FRAU

VERBS

28

Actions speak louder than words. Here is a list of common verbs you might encounter.

P	M	E	S	E	E	E	G	N	A	H	C	O	T	H
E	T	W	T	E	E	B	E	R	A	E	H	O	T	N
E	M	O	M	E	I	L	O	K	O	O	C	O	T	E
L	E	E	P	E	H	N	E	T	R	A	W	O	N	F
S	D	T	P	A	E	L	A	I	R	T	S	I	T	A
O	N	F	Z	G	Y	L	I	R	T	I	A	O	R	L
T	Y	E	A	H	K	P	Y	T	N	N	R	E	A	H
O	B	R	G	O	N	R	A	G	R	E	T	T	G	C
T	F	A	C	L	T	E	O	T	A	L	O	O	E	S
H	N	H	N	T	O	E	S	D	E	A	S	W	N	I
I	E	H	L	T	H	F	G	S	S	S	E	A	T	N
N	R	E	D	N	Ä	C	E	K	E	O	E	I	C	G
K	Ö	N	O	D	V	N	U	I	P	F	E	T	R	E
D	H	N	R	C	O	S	R	Ä	D	E	N	K	E	N
S	S	E	H	E	N	T	O	F	O	L	L	O	W	S

TO ASK	FRAGEN
TO BE	SEIN
TO CARRY	TRAGEN
TO CHANGE	ÄNDERN
TO COOK	KOCHEN
TO EAT	ESSEN
TO FOLLOW	FOLGEN
TO HEAR	HÖREN
TO PAY	BEZAHLEN
TO READ	LESEN
TO SEE	SEHEN
TO SING	SINGEN
TO SLEEP	SCHLAFEN
TO THINK	DENKEN
TO WAIT	WARTEN

MORE VERBS

29

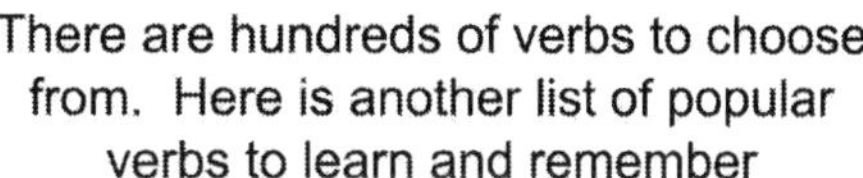

There are hundreds of verbs to choose from. Here is another list of popular verbs to learn and remember

I	S	C	H	L	I	E	ß	E	N	A	L	E	E	F
T	O	H	A	V	E	T	N	E	O	E	V	H	I	D
O	T	O	T	A	K	E	H	D	E	O	F	N	N	T
U	O	T	T	M	H	E	N	W	L	M	D	L	N	B
N	D	U	O	C	T	E	T	O	S	E	L	L	E	I
D	O	N	E	S	H	O	T	T	N	K	F	I	H	H
E	T	R	R	M	P	A	F	O	A	N	N	E	C	R
R	P	E	E	H	O	E	S	I	T	I	E	B	U	O
S	V	N	E	I	P	C	A	E	N	R	B	E	S	F
T	E	E	N	L	S	H	O	K	S	D	A	N	O	K
A	R	B	E	I	T	E	N	T	N	O	H	V	E	O
N	R	H	M	N	E	K	N	I	R	T	L	B	E	O
D	O	H	M	I	D	N	M	I	I	O	O	C	A	L
T	O	W	O	R	K	D	O	E	O	F	I	A	O	O
E	F	T	K	V	E	R	K	A	U	F	E	N	R	T

TO CLOSE	SCHLIEßEN
TO COME	KOMMEN
TO DO	TUN
TO DRINK	TRINKEN
TO FIND	FINDEN
TO HAVE	HABEN
TO HELP	HELFEN
TO LOOK FOR	SUCHEN
TO LOVE	LIEBEN
TO SELL	VERKAUFEN
TO SPEAK	SPRECHEN
TO TAKE	NEHMEN
TO TRAVEL	REISEN
TO UNDERSTAND	VERSTEHEN
TO WORK	ARBEITEN

EVEN MORE VERBS

30

To be, or not to be? To love, or not to love?
To perform any sort of action, or not to perform it?
Here is a final set of common verbs to study.

```
E C N A D O T T O B U Y M G N
T T R N T E O A T U W D T E O
O O O E E W F Y N O S T N B T
L K L P A N R O L Z W R M E E
E N W N L E F L T O E R N N L
A O T E N A E F N L R N I Y B
R W Ö N T N Y E Ö T R N R T A
N T E N T O L H A T O G I V E
W N T Ö T E O B O D I G T A B
N E O K I E F P K L A W O T O
E H I P K A U F E N N N L Y T
H E S C H U L D E N U A E R E
E G R R S T D S F H R S A A R
G N E S S I W E W O O T V I M
A N E B I E R H C S T N E I M
```

TO BE ABLE TO	KÖNNEN
TO BUY	KAUFEN
TO DANCE	TANZEN
TO GIVE	GEBEN
TO GO	GEHEN
TO KNOW	WISSEN
TO LEARN	LERNEN
TO LEAVE	ABFAHREN
TO OPEN	ÖFFNEN
TO OWE	SCHULDEN
TO PLAY	SPIELEN
TO RUN	RENNEN
TO WALK	GEHEN
TO WANT	WOLLEN
TO WRITE	SCHREIBEN

FOOD AND DRINK

31

One of the greatest pleasures of travelling to another country is sampling the local cuisine. Study this list and you may actually know what you are ordering.

S	G	G	E	H	B	R	O	W	N	S	U	G	A	R
E	S	L	M	S	C	S	I	Ä	E	B	M	T	Y	E
L	T	T	H	O	N	E	Y	M	H	O	S	E	E	D
B	I	A	F	R	U	I	T	H	L	A	Ä	Z	H	A
A	A	F	L	E	M	E	A	T	P	S	T	U	I	L
T	E	T	D	O	S	Ü	D	R	A	E	H	C	N	O
E	E	R	E	E	C	Ü	U	A	F	N	C	K	T	K
G	T	W	E	D	N	O	M	R	I	O	S	E	L	O
E	H	H	I	T	L	I	H	E	S	D	I	R	S	H
V	C	O	C	F	T	R	A	C	G	G	E	I	U	C
A	L	N	D	Ü	E	U	E	A	W	O	L	E	G	S
B	I	I	E	T	R	D	B	A	E	E	F	F	A	K
H	M	G	T	L	T	F	R	U	T	A	K	T	R	L
L	T	U	R	E	I	E	S	Ä	K	O	Ä	G	A	I
L	B	R	A	U	N	E	R	Z	U	C	K	E	R	M

BROWN SUGAR	BRAUNER ZUCKER
BUTTER	BUTTER
CHEESE	KÄSE
CHOCOLATE	SCHOKOLADE
COFFEE	KAFFEE
EGGS	EIER
FLOUR	MEHL
FRUIT	FRÜCHTE
HONEY	HONIG
MEAT	FLEISCH
MILK	MILCH
PASTA	TEIGWAREN
SUGAR	ZUCKER
TEA	TEE
VEGETABLES	GEMÜSE

FOOD AND DRINK 2

32

That was a great first course. Now it is time for the second course. Feast on this delicious group of tasteful words.

R	I	N	D	F	L	E	I	S	C	H	A	U	E	S
B	L	Ö	E	E	E	S	I	A	B	Y	H	N	T	C
C	R	T	T	K	D	U	L	F	E	D	H	E	W	H
K	N	O	U	D	C	R	Ö	T	E	R	E	T	A	W
E	T	M	T	R	O	I	R	E	F	F	E	F	P	E
A	H	I	A	C	U	R	H	P	O	R	K	E	A	I
N	H	U	H	R	N	N	G	C	O	E	S	N	C	N
S	O	A	H	S	G	M	L	F	N	P	I	T	R	E
A	I	I	B	A	K	A	E	I	N	P	E	R	C	F
K	A	B	I	E	M	A	R	I	O	E	R	I	T	L
I	A	R	E	B	T	A	E	I	E	P	U	C	B	E
D	I	E	R	E	G	L	E	T	N	J	O	E	D	I
O	O	A	T	R	R	W	A	S	S	E	R	T	N	S
I	Ö	D	A	S	Z	L	A	S	T	C	M	O	U	C
L	A	M	M	F	L	E	I	S	C	H	T	O	T	H

BEEF	RINDFLEISCH
BEER	BIER
BREAD	BROT
CHICKEN	HUHN
JUICE	SAFT
LAMB	LAMMFLEISCH
MARGARINE	MARGARINE
OIL	ÖL
PEPPER	PFEFFER
PORK	SCHWEINEFLEISCH
RICE	REIS
SALT	SALZ
STEAK	STEAK
WATER	WASSER

FOOD AND DRINK 3

33

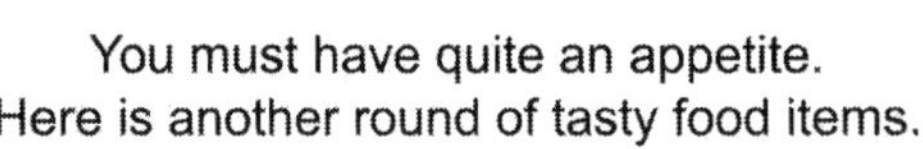

You must have quite an appetite.
Here is another round of tasty food items.

```
E N H A S E R U A S A W E I N
Y N E L A E V A O O A D O M O
D R H A L T S L B K C U D O U
L E G A B N E O K B E O O L C
K T S T S E A R O G I E C A M
A U E S D K I I U G A T T S A
L P A K A N I N C H E N D S P
B E I K G L Y O O T E N S E L
F J G E T I E R H R T E I S E
L M L Ü I H N M U U R S C W S
E A E S L S N N R G U O R T Y
I H T N I F C K S O H F E D R
S O U R C R E A M Y G I A H U
C R U E S Y G G E U O O M N P
H P O U L T R Y E E J E H N R
```

BAGEL	KRINGEL
COCOA	KAKAO
CREAM	SAHNE
DUCK	ENTE
GOOSE	GANS
MAPLE SYRUP	AHORNSIRUP
MOLASSES	MELASSE
POULTRY	GEFLÜGEL
RABBIT	KANINCHEN
SOUR CREAM	SAURE SAHNE
TURKEY	PUTER
VEAL	KALBFLEISCH
YOGURT	JOGHURT
WINE	WEIN

FRUITS

34

An apple a day keeps the dentist away. Apparently, dentists are terrified of apples. Who knows who else you might be able to scare away if you try a daily dose of these other fruits.

O T H E I D E L B E E R E N E
N P T N A L P G G E E U E I R
W I N E M U A L F P A B N S E
W N E R E E B D R E U E R M E
A E O R A N G E V A S N I U B
S A G L E G N A R O A G B L L
S P R H E E E T K G R O I P U
E P A N C M N I O A I M T R E
R L P P I I R O P C E N S R B
M E E L E P S E R T I A E S E
E M F W A A F R T T N R T E R
L O R O N R C E I A I D P P R
O N U W U H E H N F W Z L A I
N R I I T A R A E P P S G R E
E S T R A W B E R R I E S G S

APRICOT	APRIKOSE
BLUEBERRIES	HEIDELBEEREN
EGGPLANT	AUBERGINE
GRAPEFRUIT	GRAPEFRUIT
GRAPES	WEINTRAUBEN
LEMON	ZITRONE
LIME	LIMETTE
ORANGE	ORANGE
PEACH	PFIRSICH
PEAR	BIRNE
PINEAPPLE	ANANAS
PLUMS	PFLAUMEN
STRAWBERRIES	ERDBEEREN
WATERMELON	WASSERMELONE

FRUITS - PART 2

35

A fruit is the part of a plant that surrounds the seeds, whereas a vegetable is a plant that has some other edible part. There are several fruit that we often assume to be vegetables and vice versa.

R	A	K	I	R	P	A	P	R	E	N	Ü	R	G	U
E	A	I	A	N	E	R	E	E	B	M	O	R	B	E
P	H	S	G	L	B	I	C	F	R	I	A	E	B	T
P	E	I	P	A	E	U	N	B	A	N	A	N	A	A
E	F	L	N	B	C	F	S	I	A	I	E	I	G	N
P	T	A	P	U	E	I	P	T	H	H	E	K	U	A
N	N	A	M	P	B	R	A	A	C	C	T	P	R	R
E	F	B	M	R	A	P	R	S	U	C	C	M	K	G
E	E	E	Ü	O	F	R	R	I	U	U	W	U	E	E
R	E	K	I	E	T	I	E	E	E	Z	O	P	Z	M
G	W	E	L	G	K	Y	A	T	B	S	L	O	V	O
H	I	M	B	E	E	R	E	N	O	L	L	R	P	P
E	N	M	O	O	A	S	E	I	R	R	E	H	C	C
T	O	M	A	T	O	E	O	L	H	D	Y	G	R	E
T	E	T	S	E	I	R	R	E	B	K	C	A	L	B

APPLE	APFEL
BANANA	BANANE
BLACKBERRIES	BROMBEEREN
CHERRIES	KIRSCHEN
CUCUMBER	GURKE
FIG	FEIGE
GREEN PEPPER	GRÜNER PAPRIKA
POMEGRANATE	GRANATAPFEL
PUMPKIN	KÜRBIS
RASPBERRIES	HIMBEEREN
RED pepper	ROTER paprika
TOMATO	TOMATE
YELLOW pepper	GELBER paprika
ZUCCHINI	ZUCCHINI

VEGETABLES

36

Vegetables are filled with vitamins and minerals that are part of a healthy diet. Here is a list of some common vegetables that you know you should eat more often

G	S	D	D	C	A	U	L	I	F	L	O	W	E	R
I	L	O	C	C	O	R	B	E	H	B	I	L	A	D
L	E	R	O	S	E	N	K	O	H	L	E	D	O	R
E	S	S	D	Y	S	O	K	H	O	C	I	A	I	A
F	S	W	U	I	H	N	C	C	S	E	N	O	N	H
F	U	E	E	C	E	A	C	H	S	I	H	E	L	C
O	R	E	I	M	N	O	R	C	L	C	D	E	F	S
T	B	T	U	I	R	G	H	U	K	E	E	A	E	S
R	R	L	P	B	A	E	G	A	T	K	N	N	R	I
A	B	S	R	R	N	I	P	L	S	A	H	N	N	W
K	O	H	L	R	Ü	B	E	B	ß	O	B	O	E	S
ß	N	I	Y	O	H	C	K	O	B	W	A	A	N	F
Ü	C	N	ß	Y	E	M	A	N	G	O	L	D	G	R
S	P	I	N	A	T	M	E	K	L	A	U	C	H	A
W	I	I	N	A	R	T	I	S	C	H	O	C	K	E

ARTICHOKE	ARTISCHOCKE
BOK CHOY	PAK-CHOI
BROCCOLI	BROCCOLI
BRUSSELS sprouts	ROSENKOHL
CAULIFLOWER	BLUMENKOHL
FENNEL	FENCHEL
GARLIC	KNOBLAUCH
green BEAN	grüne BOHNE
LEEKS	LAUCH
RADISH	RADIESCHEN
RUTABAGA	KOHLRÜBE
SPINACH	SPINAT
SWEET potato	SÜßKARTOFFEL
SWISS CHARD	MANGOLD

VEGETABLES 2

37

Vegetables come in all shapes and colours.
Here is another list of nutritious veggies.

S	L	Ü	P	A	R	S	N	I	P	E	N	O	L	S
R	T	K	N	G	Y	K	A	I	T	A	D	E	I	A
Ü	E	A	O	E	R	R	N	E	S	O	B	A	Z	L
B	P	R	N	S	S	R	E	P	P	E	R	U	L	A
E	O	O	I	G	U	B	A	L	I	N	C	R	I	T
K	T	T	O	T	E	R	R	W	E	K	E	I	A	S
A	A	T	N	T	A	N	Z	E	E	C	O	E	E	C
R	T	E	O	G	O	E	S	R	E	S	S	L	R	E
T	O	R	U	L	C	L	E	E	N	N	B	E	S	G
O	E	S	L	U	A	R	L	O	L	A	Ü	Ü	N	A
F	S	B	T	H	B	H	W	A	T	L	M	R	T	B
F	A	T	E	S	O	P	C	E	H	E	E	C	G	B
E	E	R	E	F	E	K	G	S	G	S	T	R	S	A
L	R	N	B	A	L	E	G	R	A	P	S	N	I	C
N	A	S	S	I	V	P	A	S	T	I	N	A	K	E

ASPARAGUS	SPARGEL
BEET	ROTE BEETE
CABBAGE	KOHL
CARROT	KAROTTE
CELERY	STANGENSELLERIE
GREEN PEAS	GRÜNE ERBSEN
LETTUCE	SALAT
ONION	ZWIEBEL
PARSNIP	PASTINAKE
POTATOES	KARTOFFELN
SHALLOT	SCHALOTTE
SNOW PEAS	ZUCKERERBSEN
TURNIP	RÜBE
VEGETABLES	GEMÜSE

SEAFOOD

38

If you happen to be travelling near the coast, be sure to stop in at a local restaurant and try the local fresh fish and shellfish. Here is a list of some edible sea creatures that might find their way into your belly.

D	N	L	E	H	C	S	U	M	S	U	N	E	V	Y
A	O	O	R	K	E	S	W	H	A	L	I	B	U	T
O	E	E	M	A	I	I	S	L	E	S	S	U	M	H
E	E	L	L	L	O	S	L	H	A	A	M	E	W	U
K	L	L	N	M	A	E	C	B	H	N	A	P	R	N
A	E	O	R	A	R	S	E	A	U	R	L	O	E	F
M	N	H	T	R	U	S	H	E	L	T	C	T	M	I
M	R	C	H	M	I	D	O	C	R	L	T	P	M	S
M	A	S	H	H	E	R	U	L	A	R	O	B	U	C
U	G	N	D	O	E	R	E	D	E	L	O	P	H	H
S	V	S	U	T	V	E	D	T	S	B	O	O	E	M
C	T	A	S	T	Y	Y	S	Q	Y	T	B	T	E	N
H	L	B	A	R	C	U	U	N	C	E	K	A	R	K
E	O	T	E	L	A	I	D	O	Y	S	T	E	R	S
L	E	L	L	E	D	R	A	S	H	R	I	M	P	K

ANCHOVY	SARDELLE
CLAMS	VENUSMUSCHELN
CRAB	KRABBE
EEL	AAL
HALIBUT	HEILBUTT
LOBSTER	HUMMER
MUSSELS	MUSCHELN
OCTOPUS	KRAKE
OYSTERS	AUSTER
SALMON	LACHS
SCALLOP	KAMMMUSCHEL
SHRIMP	GARNELE
SOLE	SCHOLLE
SQUID	KALMAR
TUNA	THUNFISCH

HERBS

39

Here is a list of herbs that can be used to
add some flavour to your meals.
Variety is the essence of life, so give them a try.

R	E	D	N	A	I	R	O	C	L	A	N	S	H	E
E	O	Y	R	A	M	E	S	O	R	A	R	A	L	A
I	I	T	L	R	C	D	U	O	T	E	R	V	L	N
L	T	I	O	S	E	N	N	I	T	E	T	O	I	D
I	T	H	Y	M	I	A	N	U	E	A	S	R	D	E
S	P	A	O	S	G	I	Ä	B	E	B	A	Y	E	M
R	W	A	T	E	E	R	R	S	R	M	L	E	G	U
E	W	E	R	E	K	O	N	E	S	E	I	A	A	K
T	S	O	E	S	L	K	H	O	S	I	N	N	S	I
E	B	T	H	T	L	O	R	I	G	A	N	O	T	L
P	E	A	R	D	B	E	N	M	H	A	S	A	L	I
P	M	E	S	A	D	A	Y	I	A	W	R	R	R	S
W	Y	P	G	I	G	D	Y	N	E	N	S	R	E	A
Ä	H	N	L	U	L	O	I	Z	F	X	H	A	A	B
S	T	L	B	B	O	H	N	E	N	K	R	A	U	T

ANISE	ANIS
BASIL	BASILIKUM
CORIANDER	KORIANDER
DILL	DILL
HERBS	KRÄUTER
MINT	MINZE
OREGANO	ORIGANO
PARSLEY	PETERSILIE
ROSEMARY	ROSMARIN
SAGE	SALBEI
SAVORY	BOHNENKRAUT
SWEET BAY	LORBEER
TARRAGON	ESTRAGON
THYME	THYMIAN

AROUND THE HOUSE

40

Home is where the heart is.
It is also where you keep all of your stuff.
Review the following common household terms.

H	C	A	D	H	I	F	M	D	D	F	E	K	M	E
S	R	E	L	L	E	K	A	I	I	O	Ü	O	Y	R
C	W	I	N	D	O	W	N	A	T	O	O	A	A	D
H	F	E	S	S	Z	I	M	M	E	R	W	S	E	H
L	B	L	A	W	N	A	I	H	H	E	E	B	B	Z
A	A	E	A	G	G	V	A	T	V	N	E	A	R	U
F	L	F	R	U	G	A	A	I	S	W	S	L	E	F
Z	K	O	E	A	N	B	R	N	A	E	U	C	M	A
I	O	Ü	R	N	E	D	E	A	M	O	O	O	M	R
M	N	A	C	T	S	H	R	E	G	S	H	N	I	H
M	G	T	T	H	C	T	N	Y	W	E	U	Y	Z	T
E	N	E	S	T	E	T	E	A	R	H	A	A	N	S
R	T	L	I	V	I	N	G	R	O	O	M	D	H	W
C	R	K	O	G	Ü	B	E	D	R	O	O	M	O	E
W	W	A	S	C	H	K	Ü	C	H	E	S	M	W	G

BALCONY	BALKON
BASEMENT	KELLER
BATHROOM	WC
BED	BETT
BEDROOM	SCHLAFZIMMER
DINING ROOM	ESSZIMMER
DRIVEWAY	ZUFARHTSWEG
GARAGE	GARAGE
HOUSE	HAUS
KITCHEN	KÜCHE
LAUNDRY ROOM	WASCHKÜCHE
LAWN	RASEN
LIVING ROOM	WOHNZIMMER
ROOF	DACH
WINDOW	FENSTER

AROUND THE HOUSE 2

41

Home, home on the range, where the deer and the antelope play. Why are those stupid deer and antelope always playing Frisbee on my lawn? Here are some more house terms.

```
R S C H W I M M B E C K E N I
S W F N I M A K E E U P C U E
N U A Z O V O R H A N G R E A
K E W S I A H C S I T L E L E
R I O T H Z T I A V O O S B C
O V B T L E W T S O T W S A H
N G A A F I R E P L A C E T A
L L T E D U G U I S M D R A N
E Ü H S C E A H S S O E D F D
U H T E R B W E T M I F O A E
C L U V R P R A M B L T A U L
H A B O S H O O N O U E Z C I
T M V L A O K R A N I L T E E
E P S H T I F E C N E F B T R
R E N I H C S A M H C S A W A
```

BATHTUB	BADEWANNE
CHANDELIER	KRONLEUCHTER
CURTAIN	VORHANG
DRESSER	KOMMODE
FAUCET	WASSERHAHN
FENCE	ZAUN
FIREPLACE	KAMIN
LIGHT BULB	GLÜHLAMPE
LOVESEAT	ZWEISITZER
POOL	SCHWIMMBECKEN
PORCH	VORBAU
SOFA	SOFA
TABLE	TISCH
WASHER	WASCHMASCHINE

AROUND THE HOUSE 3

42

Here is a list of some more common household items and modern conveniences.

K L E I D E R S C H R A N K N
G A K A N A R M C H A I R D S
R A N N S S T E P P E R T U A
E E R I A E P F I T N T S S R
F R N D S R H I S G E I H C M
R K I O E A H N E B K O O H L
I I L O L R R C R G C E W E E
G C A L M O O E S H E I E L H
E R N H H R T B S L B L R E N
R I O C C T A T E I H E O I S
A B S R I H U L D A C Ü D D T
T T I G R H G E A N S D K E U
O E I D L I T I S T A I R S H
R V E Y E N M I H C W O H K L
S H C S I T B I E R H C S F T

ARMCHAIR	ARMLEHNSTUHL
ARMOIRE	KLEIDERSCHRANK
BIDET	BIDET
CHIMNEY	SCHORNSTEIN
CLOSET	GARDEROBE
CRIB	GITTERBETT
DESK	SCHREIBTISCH
HALL	DIELE
HIGH CHAIR	HOCHSTUHL
MIRROR	SPIEGEL
REFRIGERATOR	KÜHLSCHRANK
SHOWER	DUSCHE
SINK	WASCHBECKEN
STAIRS	TREPPE

AT THE TABLE

4 3

Table setting etiquette dictates that the forks be placed on the left hand side of the plate, and knives on the right. Here are some items you might find on your table - probably in the wrong location.

N	O	O	P	S	E	L	B	A	T	S	U	G	A	R
E	A	Ü	T	E	A	P	O	T	G	I	W	S	S	P
R	S	P	D	T	T	L	S	A	L	A	D	T	L	F
E	R	O	K	F	F	A	Z	W	S	A	L	E	N	E
S	E	E	D	I	O	L	L	S	E	G	S	A	O	F
S	P	F	I	R	N	R	E	P	T	S	L	K	O	F
E	P	I	H	E	E	R	K	F	Ü	R	W	A	P	E
M	E	N	F	H	K	K	T	H	F	E	E	W	S	R
N	P	K	C	R	L	E	C	I	K	Ö	G	U	A	S
O	P	T	U	E	E	S	O	U	R	E	L	L	E	T
O	I	G	B	K	T	I	D	H	Z	I	A	S	T	R
P	A	A	A	A	L	E	F	F	Ö	L	S	S	E	E
S	G	N	L	E	T	T	E	I	V	R	E	S	M	U
E	N	A	E	L	E	F	F	Ö	L	E	E	T	Ü	E
E	S	G	R	E	S	S	E	M	K	A	E	T	S	R

FORK	GABEL
GLASS	GLAS
KNIFE	MESSER
NAPKIN	SERVIETTE
PEPPER shaker	PFEFFERSTREUER
PLATE	TELLER
SALAD bowl	SALATSCHÜSSEL
SALT shaker	SALZSTREUER
SPOON	LÖFFEL
STEAK knife	STEAKMESSER
SUGAR bowl	ZUCKERDOSE
TABLESPOON	ESSLÖFFEL
TEAPOT	TEEKANNE
TEASPOON	TEELÖFFEL
water PITCHER	WASSERKRUG

TOOLS

44

Whether you're a regular handyman or a DIY disaster waiting to happen, here are some basic tools that you should have lying around somewhere.

M	I	E	S	T	H	O	L	Z	H	A	M	M	E	R
A	E	T	I	Ä	S	L	E	S	S	Ü	L	H	C	S
A	U	N	A	A	O	N	Y	R	E	T	O	I	C	Ä
N	L	M	U	T	T	E	R	N	E	M	U	H	N	N
V	E	D	L	A	E	B	Z	Ä	I	D	R	G	S	A
R	G	F	Ü	P	L	U	A	T	X	A	D	C	H	R
D	A	R	G	E	L	A	N	R	U	B	R	A	Ä	P
D	N	O	N	M	A	R	G	B	I	E	M	G	L	C
H	N	A	E	E	M	H	E	A	W	M	A	I	E	L
R	C	O	B	A	C	C	N	D	E	N	E	N	E	T
W	S	N	Ü	S	S	S	R	R	A	R	I	I	Ä	Ü
E	R	Ä	E	U	S	I	A	I	S	S	T	L	O	B
R	R	I	G	R	V	E	L	W	I	E	A	E	E	E
C	Ä	A	N	E	W	Ä	M	T	R	E	M	M	A	H
S	C	H	R	A	U	B	E	N	Z	I	E	H	E	R

BOLTS	SCHRAUBEN
HAMMER	HAMMER
LADDER	LEITER
MALLET	HOLZHAMMER
NAIL	NAGEL
NUTS	MUTTERN
PLIERS	ZANGEN
SAW	SÄGE
SCREW	SCHRAUBE
SCREWDRIVER	SCHRAUBENZIEHER
TAPE MEASURE	MESSBAND
WRENCH	SCHLÜSSEL

CLOTHING

45

Fashion can be comfortable, sexy, strange or just plain weird. Whatever category your style falls into, here are some clothing items you can use to study and cover up with.

P	A	N	T	S	T	R	U	M	P	F	H	O	S	E
U	Ü	S	H	S	T	N	T	A	H	C	H	E	C	O
S	A	H	T	O	E	O	S	F	Y	E	V	S	H	E
E	T	O	H	C	M	H	C	H	O	O	F	H	U	Y
B	W	R	K	K	O	E	G	K	L	E	I	D	H	M
A	I	T	L	E	B	Ü	T	G	I	E	T	R	E	H
D	I	S	S	N	R	P	J	E	O	N	O	A	H	A
E	S	E	T	T	A	W	A	R	K	T	G	S	A	N
M	O	A	E	R	E	V	C	N	C	C	P	Y	R	D
A	C	L	M	S	O	F	K	V	T	N	A	M	D	S
N	K	E	T	A	E	H	E	O	A	Y	M	J	R	C
T	S	E	H	L	J	S	S	S	H	L	H	E	E	H
E	B	O	R	H	T	A	B	O	O	U	T	O	S	U
L	S	S	T	R	U	M	P	F	N	H	T	T	S	H
G	U	Z	N	A	F	A	L	H	C	S	O	E	C	E

BATHROBE	BADEMANTEL
BELT	GÜRTEL
DRESS	KLEID
GLOVES	HANDSCHUHE
HAT	HUT
JACKET	JACKE
NECKTIE	KRAWATTE
PAJAMAS	SCHLAFANZUG
PANTS	HOSE
PANTY HOSE	STRUMPFHOSE
SHOES	SCHUHE
SHORTS	SHORTS
SOCKS	SOCKEN
STOCKING	STRUMPF
VEST	WESTE

MORE CLOTHING

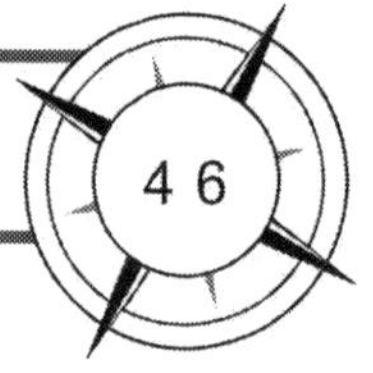

Take a look inside your closet for these clothing items. The 70s called, and they want that shirt back.

E	S	D	E	S	R	E	D	N	E	P	S	U	S	L
H	T	G	S	E	T	P	U	H	L	E	N	B	O	E
C	I	D	P	R	H	U	R	A	I	N	C	O	A	T
S	F	E	I	R	B	G	N	I	H	T	O	L	C	N
Ä	W	K	L	A	H	E	M	D	A	E	R	Ä	A	A
W	S	I	S	A	N	D	A	L	E	N	M	T	E	M
R	N	O	M	B	L	O	U	S	E	R	R	K	S	N
E	A	B	I	S	A	T	S	G	U	I	W	L	E	E
T	E	U	T	T	U	D	E	B	H	I	A	E	E	G
N	J	O	R	I	R	I	E	S	G	D	T	I	A	E
U	O	I	C	E	L	I	T	A	N	U	T	D	S	R
B	H	S	S	F	E	E	H	A	N	W	Z	U	A	K
S	S	S	J	E	A	N	S	S	O	Z	L	N	S	C
E	W	A	H	L	O	O	S	B	T	B	U	G	A	O
U	S	E	E	H	O	S	E	N	T	R	Ä	G	E	R

BLOUSE	BLUSE
BOOTS	STIEFEL
BOW TIE	FLIEGE
BRIEFS	SLIP
CLOTHING	KLEIDUNG
JEANS	JEANS
RAINCOAT	REGENMANTEL
SANDALS	SANDALEN
SHIRT	HEMD
SKIRT	ROCK
SUIT	ANZUG
SUSPENDERS	HOSENTRÄGER
SWIM SUIT	BADEANZUG
T-SHIRT	T-SHIRT
UNDERWEAR	UNTERWÄSCHE

JEWELS & ACCESSORIES

47

Jewellery has been around for millennia. Precious metals and gemstones are used to make beautiful and intricate designs that please the eye and hurt the wallet. Here are some jewellery terms to dazzle you.

S	D	L	A	R	E	M	E	Ä	N	E	B	E	H	Y
G	G	E	A	L	Ä	G	T	O	P	A	Z	R	H	B
T	N	N	O	P	O	F	N	N	A	N	E	U	B	U
S	E	I	I	W	O	T	R	I	A	T	D	B	Y	R
S	L	K	R	R	N	B	S	E	R	M	N	I	W	T
L	R	T	C	A	R	A	C	E	G	R	A	N	G	N
R	E	C	D	O	P	A	L	W	E	N	H	I	E	O
A	P	N	S	P	L	D	E	B	A	H	Ä	O	D	L
E	E	C	H	K	G	I	R	T	E	T	E	H	D	L
P	H	I	C	A	S	A	P	H	I	R	C	O	N	I
E	R	E	R	S	C	M	O	A	I	O	R	H	A	A
E	N	A	I	E	D	O	L	N	O	N	I	S	B	D
E	M	T	L	O	R	N	G	R	H	U	G	N	M	E
S	P	E	T	E	N	D	B	T	O	P	A	S	R	M
E	T	T	E	K	S	L	A	H	R	T	C	R	A	I

BRACELET	ARMBAND
BROOCH	BROSCHE
DIAMOND	DIAMANT
EARRINGS	OHRRINGE
EMERALD	SMARAGD
LOCKET	MEDAILLON
NECKLACE	HALSKETTE
OPAL	OPAL
PEARLS	PERLEN
PENDANT	ANHÄNGER
RING	RING
RUBY	RUBIN
SAPPHIRE	SAPHIR
TOPAZ	TOPAS
WATCH	UHR

TOILETRIES

48

Here are some of the everyday items you use to make yourself presentable to the outside world. Some people may need more than others....

R	K	O	N	T	A	K	T	L	I	N	S	E	N	D
R	K	V	N	A	F	L	O	S	S	Z	R	A	O	E
R	A	Z	O	R	E	I	O	S	A	C	E	N	N	O
Y	M	A	O	A	T	E	T	H	E	N	O	C	D	D
C	M	H	P	P	C	N	N	S	L	S	L	M	H	O
O	Z	N	M	P	H	B	A	I	N	I	N	A	B	R
N	A	P	A	A	Ü	H	P	R	P	E	A	E	O	A
D	H	A	H	R	R	S	S	P	O	R	P	O	L	N
I	N	S	S	E	T	E	E	U	S	D	P	P	L	T
T	S	T	A	I	T	R	Y	P	R	M	O	A	I	N
I	E	A	C	S	S	E	Ü	R	A	B	D	E	Ö	L
O	I	K	A	A	W	L	L	H	D	E	I	F	D	E
N	D	P	O	R	U	H	S	A	W	H	T	U	O	M
E	E	S	V	N	R	E	S	S	A	W	D	N	U	M
R	N	A	G	E	L	K	N	I	P	S	E	R	A	O

COMB	KAMM
CONDITIONER	HAARSPÜLUNG
contact LENSES	KONTAKTLINSEN
dental FLOSS	ZAHNSEIDE
DEODORANT	DEODORANT
hair DRYER	FÖN
LIPSTICK	LIPPENSTIFT
MOUTHWASH	MUNDWASSER
nail CLIPPERS	NAGELKNIPSER
RAZOR	RASIERAPPARAT
SHAMPOO	SHAMPOO
toothBRUSH	ZAHNBÜRSTE
toothPASTE	ZAHNPASTA

SPORTS

49

Whether you are a professional athlete,
or an armchair quarterback, here is a list of
sports from around the world that you can cheer for.

L	N	E	N	R	U	T	E	T	Ä	R	E	G	V	L
E	O	E	S	W	B	A	S	E	B	A	L	L	O	E
I	I	O	X	A	E	O	F	U	ß	B	A	L	L	I
P	L	S	C	O	G	I	X	I	U	T	O	Y	L	P
S	N	N	K	E	B	Y	T	I	R	E	G	E	E	S
L	C	I	E	U	L	E	M	O	N	N	O	K	Y	L
L	G	H	Ä	G	N	L	P	N	I	G	Ä	C	B	L
A	N	T	W	N	N	S	A	L	A	F	C	O	A	A
B	I	G	I	I	T	I	T	B	E	S	S	H	L	B
Y	C	S	H	H	M	S	R	L	T	K	T	S	L	T
E	N	E	C	I	E	M	T	E	A	E	U	I	O	E
L	E	E	S	R	E	T	E	T	C	U	K	E	C	K
L	F	S	W	I	M	M	I	N	G	C	F	S	I	S
O	E	T	R	T	E	N	N	I	S	A	O	H	A	A
V	R	H	R	D	G	Y	L	L	A	B	E	S	A	B

BASEBALL	BASEBALL
BASKETBALL	BASKETBALLSPIEL
BOXING	BOXEN
FENCING	FECHTSPORT
figure SKATING	EISKUNSTLAUF
GYMNASTICS	GERÄTETURNEN
ICE hockey	EISHOCKEY
SOCCER	FUßBALL
SWIMMING	SCHWIMMEN
TENNIS	TENNIS
VOLLEYBALL	VOLLEYBALLSPIEL
WRESTLING	RINGEN

MORE SPORTS

50

Soccer and cricket are two of the most popular sports in the world. Here are some more sports for you to try and suck at.

E	N	E	G	N	I	R	P	S	T	S	N	U	K	W
G	F	N	I	L	E	V	A	J	P	I	G	T	A	E
S	N	U	E	W	L	U	G	E	N	N	N	S	G	I
I	A	U	A	T	T	E	E	S	O	N	S	A	N	S
N	G	E	R	L	T	D	D	L	M	E	S	C	U	S
N	S	N	H	P	G	I	G	O	R	T	K	R	R	C
E	B	I	U	T	S	N	L	B	R	A	I	I	P	H
T	G	O	O	R	I	H	A	H	E	N	I	C	S	N
H	C	G	B	V	P	L	C	L	C	Y	N	K	I	E
C	R	S	I	S	L	S	V	O	I	S	G	E	E	L
S	I	D	P	S	L	A	H	O	H	K	B	T	R	L
I	C	A	P	E	U	E	L	C	S	B	S	O	D	L
T	K	I	O	L	E	O	D	T	O	O	A	R	B	A
W	E	I	T	S	P	R	U	N	G	H	N	T	E	U
L	T	R	I	P	L	E	O	H	S	E	Y	D	S	F

BOBSLED
CRICKET
cross country SKIING
DIVING
HIGH jump
JAVELIN
LONG jump
LUGE
pole VAULT
SPEED skating
table TENNIS
TRIPLE jump
water POLO

BOBSCHLITTEN
CRICKET
SKILANGLAUF
KUNSTSPRINGEN
HOCHSPRUNG
SPEER
WEITSPRUNG
RENNRODEL
STABHOCHSPRUNG
EISSCHNELLLAUF
TISCHTENNIS
DREISPRUNG
WASSERBALLSPIEL

PLACES

51

Here is a list of places that you might visit on a daily, weekly or monthly basis. There are some places on this list that you probably want to avoid.

M	O	V	I	E	T	H	E	A	T	E	R	A	B	T
E	U	A	E	T	R	O	P	R	I	A	T	T	M	E
C	C	I	H	S	U	A	H	N	E	K	N	A	R	K
I	A	I	D	M	U	S	E	U	M	E	S	H	U	R
F	E	T	F	A	T	O	N	T	M	S	C	O	T	A
F	L	M	H	F	T	F	H	T	O	O	H	S	T	M
O	O	U	Ü	E	O	S	R	T	D	I	U	P	H	R
T	O	S	G	W	D	A	T	I	H	P	L	I	C	E
S	H	E	G	H	P	R	O	M	E	G	E	T	U	P
O	C	U	E	E	A	B	A	R	A	D	I	A	E	U
P	S	M	D	D	A	F	M	L	Ü	T	H	L	L	S
E	K	C	Ü	R	B	A	E	O	D	B	S	O	N	I
N	E	G	D	I	R	B	E	N	K	I	N	O	F	S
R	O	D	F	K	A	U	F	H	A	U	S	B	P	D
Y	R	A	T	E	M	E	C	N	O	I	D	A	T	S

AIRPORT	FLUGHAFEN
BAR	BAR
BRIDGE	BRÜCKE
CATHEDRAL	DOM
CEMETARY	FRIEDHOF
DEPARTMENT store	KAUFHAUS
HOSPITAL	KRANKENHAUS
LIGHTHOUSE	LEUCHTTURM
MOVIE THEATER	KINO
MUSEUM	MUSEUM
OFFICE	BÜRO
POST OFFICE	POSTAMT
SCHOOL	SCHULE
STADIUM	STADION
SUPERMARKET	SUPERMARKT

MORE PLACES

52

The weekend is finally here. Where do you feel like going tonight? Here are some more places you can visit.

E	H	E	O	U	N	I	V	E	R	S	I	T	Ä	T
G	K	L	A	P	O	T	H	E	K	E	N	N	D	N
Q	G	R	C	E	E	P	A	R	K	P	L	A	T	Z
T	H	E	A	T	E	R	F	L	D	K	T	R	R	K
P	A	T	S	P	K	H	N	O	T	S	R	U	N	C
A	R	A	T	C	E	D	W	H	N	E	V	A	I	U
R	B	E	L	N	H	N	T	E	A	E	B	T	P	N
K	O	H	E	H	T	Ä	N	H	R	U	Y	S	P	I
I	R	T	O	O	O	N	F	O	U	H	S	E	C	V
N	K	T	W	B	I	T	T	T	A	A	U	R	H	E
G	E	N	U	U	L	S	E	L	T	F	A	D	R	R
L	Y	R	A	R	B	I	L	L	S	E	H	A	R	S
O	G	T	M	B	I	F	L	Y	E	N	T	O	A	I
T	N	Y	E	Y	B	P	H	A	R	M	A	C	Y	T
S	E	S	U	O	H	A	R	E	P	O	R	A	O	Y

BANK	BANK
CASTLE	BURG
CITY HALL	RATHAUS
DOWNTOWN	INNENSTADT
HARBOR	HAFEN
HOTEL	HOTEL
LIBRARY	BIBLIOTHEK
OPERA HOUSE	OPERNHAUS
PARK	PARK
PARKING LOT	PARKPLATZ
PHARMACY	APOTHEKE
RESTAURANT	RESTAURANT
STORE	GESCHÄFT
THEATER	THEATER
UNIVERSITY	UNIVERSITÄT

EVEN MORE PLACES

53

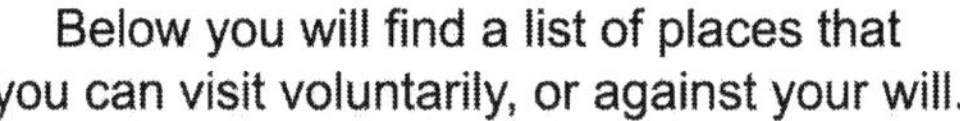

Below you will find a list of places that
you can visit voluntarily, or against your will.


```
H A B O W L I N G B A H N D N
R M L O T B H L G S L V P A O
E T U D O A U O E U Q S O M I
I Q M F B K L S M B Y E A M T
V A E U S F S O B N H D E R A
E S N U P F S T A A G R D A T
R D L L G C O G O N H É Z I S
I A A A H O O H I R F N D L E
E T D E W G G L N A E E H R R
Z F E U E R W A C H E W C O I
I D N R H O E T N F A I R A F
L F S U B W A Y F Y O B U D G
O L E E A F L O R I S T H T B
P O L I C E C S R K I R C H E
O G G N U L D N A H H C U B R
```

BOOKSTORE	BUCHHANDLUNG
BOWLING alley	BOWLINGBAHN
BUS station	BUSBAHNHOF
CHURCH	KIRCHE
COFFEE shop	CAFÉ
DAM	DAMM
FIRE STATION	FEUERWACHE
FLORIST	BLUMENLADEN
GOLF course	GOLFPLATZ
MOSQUE	MOSCHEE
POLICE station	POLIZEIREVIER
RAILROAD station	BAHNHOF
SUBWAY station	U-BAHN-station
SYNAGOGUE	SYNAGOGE

ON THE ROAD

54

Here are some vehicles you might cross paths with on your daily commute. Please try to keep the road rage to a minimum.

E	E	N	T	F	A	U	T	O	M	O	B	I	L	E
L	A	S	T	W	A	G	E	N	A	V	I	N	I	M
B	R	ß	N	E	H	M	I	B	M	O	K	U	D	P
I	E	T	E	C	O	E	D	O	T	T	N	E	I	N
T	I	N	G	F	M	O	T	O	R	C	Y	C	L	E
R	S	T	A	T	I	O	N	A	S	K	K	I	S	G
E	E	P	W	E	R	S	R	R	A	U	S	A	M	A
V	B	V	O	R	T	T	A	B	P	V	B	P	I	W
N	U	C	A	R	M	C	R	U	S	O	U	W	A	E
O	S	D	O	O	T	I	O	U	V	K	S	S	T	D
C	E	P	P	E	O	W	N	A	C	I	H	E	B	N
O	S	E	E	L	T	D	A	I	C	K	R	T	S	Ä
E	D	R	E	R	U	I	P	G	B	H	D	L	L	L
H	T	T	E	A	A	B	T	Ä	E	U	A	G	G	E
S	T	R	A	ß	E	N	B	A	H	N	S	N	E	G

AUTOMOBILE	AUTO
BUS	BUS
CAR	WAGEN
COACH	REISEBUS
CONVERTIBLE	KABRIOLETT
MINIVAN	MINIBUS
MOPED	MOFA
MOTORCYCLE	MOTORRAD
PICKUP truck	PICKUP
SPORTS car	SPORTWAGEN
SUV	GELÄNDEWAGEN
STATION wagon	KOMBI
STREETCAR	STRAßENBAHN
TRUCK	LASTWAGEN

VEHICLES

55

There are many means of travel you can employ to arrive at your final destination. Here is a list of various modes of transportation.

H	N	E	G	A	W	S	G	N	U	T	T	E	R	L
B	F	A	N	S	A	L	U	U	K	N	A	T	B	N
O	A	R	I	I	U	B	O	C	Z	A	E	U	U	L
O	H	E	E	R	A	B	U	O	C	A	N	O	E	Ö
T	R	T	S	H	P	R	L	N	H	T	N	U	D	S
R	R	P	N	U	T	L	T	U	E	C	E	C	U	C
G	A	O	R	E	B	U	A	R	H	C	S	B	U	H
U	D	C	R	K	U	M	S	N	N	C	N	I	E	F
E	E	I	E	I	S	E	A	A	E	E	S	C	I	A
Z	F	L	T	C	E	B	L	R	I	O	A	Y	T	H
G	L	E	A	B	I	U	I	N	I	R	T	C	D	R
U	T	H	O	O	B	L	I	A	E	N	E	L	G	Z
L	W	O	B	M	T	L	O	V	S	S	E	E	S	E
F	T	Y	A	W	B	U	S	P	A	N	Z	E	R	U
P	O	L	I	Z	E	I	F	A	H	R	Z	E	U	G

AIRPLANE	FLUGZEUG
AMBULANCE	RETTUNGSWAGEN
BICYCLE	FAHRRAD
BOAT	BOOT
CANOE	KANU
city BUS	LINIENBUS
FIRE TRUCK	LÖSCHFAHRZEUG
HELICOPTER	HUBSCHRAUBER
POLICE CAR	POLIZEIFAHRZEUG
SCHOOL bus	SCHULBUS
SUBMARINE	UNTERSEEBOOT
SUBWAY	U-BAHN
TANK	PANZER
TRAIN	ZUG

LANGUAGES

56

There are thought to be more than 3000 languages spoken around the world today. Here is a snapshot of some of the more common ones.

```
N A E R O K O R E A N I S C H
D S E E S G R I E C H I S C H
N E A M F P R A E M T H S A P
F H U C A M A N D A R I N O E
P R O T A N G N L R N I R H H
E H A U S L D I I A H T Y C T
H S C N I C E A P S U A H S C
C I E S Z N H A R G H L E I P
S L H U I Ö J C I I H I B N N
I O A S G S S E S E N A P A J
B P C O T U S I K I R N M P Ö
A H E H A I T U S A L R N S I
R N A I S S U R R C E G H O O
A I H C N E R F O G H G N T T
A K H C S I N L O P G R E E K
```

ARABIC	ARABISCH
ENGLISH	ENGLISCH
FRENCH	FRANZÖSISCH
GERMAN	DEUTSCH
GREEK	GRIECHISCH
ITALIAN	ITALIENISCH
JAPANESE	JAPANISCH
KOREAN	KOREANISCH
MANDARIN	MANDARIN
POLISH	POLNISCH
PORTUGUESE	PORTUGIESISCH
RUSSIAN	RUSSISCH
SPANISH	SPANISCH
THAI	THAI

MORE LANGUAGES

57

Here are some more popular languages from around the world. Maybe you already know one or two of them.

```
A D R H C T U D S U A H E L I
C O T S I Ä H R O M A N I A N
H C S I D E W H C S I D N I H
I C A N N V I E T N A M E S E
H N S N I E T P R U R D U H I
A E S I H N E U S B E A C H H
R U B F S R D H R R E S A C P
U F E R S E S O L K I H S S E
M I S I Ä I M Ä N S I I F I R
Ä N A W D I N A E E R S D K S
N N T E A D S N N A S E H R I
I I W E I H O C G T R I U Ü S
S S A S O D I L H R E D A T C
C C C S N B U L G A R I A N H
H H N I A B A N I U T A V D T
```

BULGARIAN	BULGARISCH
DUTCH	NIEDERLÄNDISCH
FINNISH	FINNISCH
HEBREW	HEBRÄISCH
HINDI	HINDI
INDONESIAN	INDONESISCH
PERSIAN	PERSISCH
ROMANIAN	RUMÄNISCH
SWAHILI	SUAHELI
SWEDISH	SCHWEDISCH
TURKISH	TÜRKISCH
URDU	URDU
VIETNAMESE	VIETNAMESISCH

PROFESSIONS

58

What do you want to be when you grow up? What do you want to be now that you have grown up? Here is a list of professions to consider.

P	T	S	I	R	T	A	I	H	C	Y	S	P	M	R
I	N	C	R	X	R	E	K	I	R	T	K	E	L	E
L	N	H	R	O	T	C	A	E	K	R	W	R	E	T
O	A	A	C	E	J	P	E	E	Ü	C	E	D	H	M
T	M	U	I	T	T	N	I	I	C	C	N	R	R	A
T	R	S	M	C	I	A	N	R	H	I	E	S	E	E
K	E	P	D	G	I	G	I	T	E	T	L	A	R	B
E	M	I	N	E	E	R	S	H	N	Y	R	O	E	I
T	M	E	D	N	N	A	T	E	C	C	W	N	P	E
I	I	L	I	O	N	T	P	C	H	Y	T	A	I	Z
H	Z	E	D	W	C	R	I	I	E	A	S	M	L	I
C	U	R	A	H	A	T	T	S	F	L	R	P	O	L
R	A	L	R	C	Y	E	O	E	T	E	E	T	T	O
A	T	S	I	S	C	T	Z	R	A	N	H	A	Z	P
O	D	O	T	T	E	A	C	H	E	R	O	C	H	F

ACTOR	SCHAUSPIELER
ARCHITECT	ARCHITEKT
CARPENTER	ZIMMERMANN
CHEF	KÜCHENCHEF
DENTIST	ZAHNARZT
DOCTOR	ARTZ
ELECTRICIAN	ELEKTRIKER
ENGINEER	INGENIEUR
LAWYER	RECHTSANWALT
PILOT	PILOT
POLICE officer	POLIZEIBEAMTER
PSYCHIATRIST	PSYCHIATER
TEACHER	LEHRER

SOLAR SYSTEM

Pluto may have recently been demoted from the class of planets, but it still holds a special place in our hearts. Here are some important components of our solar system.

E	N	U	S	S	O	L	A	R	S	Y	S	T	E	M
M	A	S	I	U	D	N	W	O	I	H	V	W	U	S
E	E	A	Y	N	N	N	R	E	N	O	A	I	T	I
T	J	R	O	A	O	E	F	U	L	L	M	O	O	N
S	U	M	K	R	N	O	V	L	T	E	M	D	Y	R
Y	P	C	E	U	Y	K	M	V	R	A	A	A	O	E
S	I	D	T	Q	R	O	N	C	E	S	S	T	R	T
N	T	P	T	A	N	P	U	R	T	N	U	E	E	S
E	E	H	T	D	L	R	T	A	I	L	U	A	G	N
N	R	E	P	U	Y	H	P	T	P	F	D	S	T	I
N	R	U	T	A	S	N	E	E	U	N	H	N	E	F
O	S	O	N	N	E	R	N	R	J	H	T	D	O	O
S	U	N	A	R	U	D	A	N	D	O	R	D	H	A
R	E	R	N	H	T	R	O	M	R	E	A	E	S	T
T	O	T	A	L	E	C	L	I	P	S	E	U	H	O

SOLAR SYSTEM	SONNENSYSTEM
MERCURY	MERKUR
VENUS	VENUS
EARTH	ERDE
MOON	MOND
MARS	MARS
JUPITER	JUPITER
SATURN	SATURN
URANUS	URANUS
NEPTUNE	NEPTUN
PLUTO	PLUTO
SUN	SONNE
CRATER	KRATER
FULL MOON	VOLLMOND
TOTAL ECLIPSE	totale FINSTERNIS

MUSICAL INSTRUMENTS

60

Here are some instruments that might get your foot tapping and your hands clapping.

T	M	U	N	D	H	A	R	M	O	N	I	K	A	N
A	T	E	P	M	U	R	T	F	O	E	E	C	B	O
M	B	O	S	M	U	R	D	T	L	R	N	A	U	I
B	N	A	G	R	O	E	A	R	R	Ü	K	S	T	D
O	V	O	G	M	O	M	E	A	A	K	G	L	O	R
U	I	O	M	P	B	R	T	E	O	T	W	E	E	O
R	O	E	E	U	I	I	G	R	G	C	I	D	L	C
I	L	V	R	S	G	P	D	E	O	Y	R	U	H	C
N	I	I	O	B	A	E	E	S	L	M	I	D	G	A
E	N	O	H	P	O	X	A	S	L	B	P	H	S	S
Ü	E	L	E	N	D	N	O	Y	E	A	Ü	E	G	M
A	P	I	A	N	O	T	G	P	C	L	S	E	T	N
B	O	N	G	O	S	T	U	O	H	S	N	O	O	E
W	B	E	C	K	E	N	B	B	S	O	L	L	E	C
L	H	A	R	M	O	N	I	C	A	D	N	N	S	R

ACCORDION	AKKORDEON
BAGPIPES	DUDELSACK
BONGOS	BONGOS
CELLO	CELLO
CYMBALS	BECKEN
DRUMS	TROMMELN
GUITAR	GITARRE
HARMONICA	MUNDHARMONIKA
ORGAN	ORGEL
PIANO	FLÜGEL
SAXOPHONE	SAXOPHON
TAMBOURINE	TAMBURIN
TRUMPET	TROMPETE
TUBA	TUBA
VIOLIN	VIOLINE

REVIEW: NUMBERS

61

Mix & Match: The translations in the word list below have been scrambled. Draw lines between the left and right hand columns to line up the matching words.

A	H	L	C	T	O	F	H	S	Z	S	M	A	N	T
Y	S	I	T	E	R	L	A	W	I	O	U	O	W	T
A	O	U	R	N	R	S	E	E	R	R	O	H	H	H
R	F	Ü	N	F	I	I	B	S	E	Z	U	C	T	I
I	D	I	S	D	F	E	L	T	E	L	A	O	T	R
L	O	P	F	T	N	E	T	H	V	I	E	R	F	T
N	N	R	S	T	G	W	N	G	B	H	S	V	S	E
E	E	D	Ö	I	E	E	F	I	I	E	D	R	E	E
E	N	D	Ü	L	U	E	Ü	E	T	T	H	A	N	N
T	G	R	V	N	O	E	N	H	E	Z	R	E	I	V
R	T	E	A	F	G	T	F	N	S	E	V	E	N	L
U	S	I	N	L	F	D	Z	D	N	I	L	E	O	O
O	O	T	D	Ö	I	W	E	O	I	I	X	F	O	F
F	I	P	O	W	V	T	H	R	E	E	E	A	A	E
D	R	E	I	Z	E	H	N	C	S	E	C	H	S	H

EIGHT	ACHT
ELEVEN	DREI
FIFTEEN	DREIZEHN
FIVE	EIN
FOUR	ELF
FOURTEEN	FÜNF
NINE	FÜNFZEHN
ONE	NEUN
SEVEN	SECHS
SIX	SIEBEN
TEN	VIER
THIRTEEN	VIERZEHN
THREE	ZEHN
TWELVE	ZWEI
TWO	ZWÖLF

REVIEW: NUMBERS 2

6 2

Fill-in-the-Blanks: Find the missing translations hidden in the wordsearch grid and fill-in-the-blanks in the word list below. If you need some help, refer back to the original puzzle.

T	E	I	G	H	T	E	E	N	E	S	I	X	T	Y
R	T	G	I	Z	H	C	E	S	F	I	V	E	E	P
E	H	M	T	N	H	E	Z	N	U	E	N	G	Y	T
D	O	F	I	F	T	Y	H	F	E	B	I	Y	L	U
N	U	R	S	E	V	E	N	T	Y	Z	E	T	E	O
U	S	O	N	I	Z	U	R	I	N	I	E	N	H	N
H	A	I	G	B	G	E	G	A	N	G	G	E	T	E
F	N	C	E	I	D	I	W	I	I	E	S	W	A	H
N	D	I	H	N	Z	Z	Z	G	ß	E	T	T	U	U
Ü	S	O	U	T	L	F	I	N	C	I	H	Y	S	N
F	E	H	H	L	Z	Z	N	H	U	I	E	T	E	D
T	H	C	E	Y	R	E	Z	Ü	R	E	P	R	N	R
D	A	H	A	E	E	E	H	T	F	E	N	O	D	E
A	H	E	I	G	H	T	Y	N	E	R	T	F	A	D
S	E	V	E	N	T	E	E	N	E	E	T	X	I	S

EIGHTEEN ____________
EIGHTY ____________
FIFTY ____________
FIVE hundred ____________
FORTY ____________
NINETEEN ____________
NINETY ____________
ONE HUNDRED ____________
SEVENTEEN ____________
SEVENTY ____________
SIXTEEN ____________
SIXTY ____________
THIRTY ____________
THOUSAND ____________
TWENTY ____________

REVIEW: DAYS

63

Fill-in-the-Blanks: Find the missing translations hidden in the wordsearch grid and fill-in-the-blanks in the word list below. If you need some help, refer back to the original puzzle.

W	O	C	H	E	N	E	N	D	E	S	S	E	H	L
Y	A	B	R	C	O	G	A	T	N	N	O	S	E	Y
A	A	G	A	G	O	I	F	R	I	D	A	Y	A	N
D	B	D	H	C	A	W	E	E	K	E	N	D	E	G
S	C	N	R	H	T	T	T	H	E	E	O	G	A	U
E	F	W	T	U	S	A	N	T	C	T	R	T	E	D
N	Y	Y	D	E	T	Y	G	O	I	O	S	Y	M	O
D	O	A	G	O	I	A	C	Y	M	M	W	O	E	N
E	A	O	D	E	T	D	S	W	A	T	N	E	D	N
W	N	Y	N	S	H	S	E	S	I	D	W	N	C	E
A	E	O	N	F	R	E	I	T	A	G	N	T	L	R
Y	H	E	O	L	K	U	U	Y	I	D	I	U	W	S
A	I	E	E	O	R	T	H	T	N	Y	A	S	S	T
D	W	O	R	R	O	M	O	T	E	T	L	V	E	A
O	Y	A	D	R	E	T	S	E	Y	F	B	V	E	G

________ DIENSTAG
________ DONNERSTAG
________ FREITAG
________ GESTERN
________ HEUTE
________ MITTWOCH
________ MONTAG
________ MORGEN
________ SAMSTAG
________ SONNTAG
________ TAG
________ WOCHE
________ WOCHENENDE

REVIEW: MONTHS

64

Fill-in-the-Blanks: Find the missing translations hidden in the wordsearch grid and fill-in-the-blanks in the word list below. If you need some help, refer back to the original puzzle.

R	E	B	M	E	T	P	E	S	A	L	Y	P	K	K
F	E	B	R	U	A	R	J	A	H	R	O	A	N	S
R	E	B	O	T	C	O	E	P	R	K	L	I	T	E
A	E	R	M	M	R	A	A	J	T	E	Z	L	E	P
D	E	I	A	E	H	E	U	O	N	A	I	R	H	T
N	S	O	R	E	Z	L	B	D	W	R	H	T	Ä	E
E	A	Y	C	O	Y	E	E	M	P	N	N	M	N	M
L	U	A	H	L	R	R	D	A	E	O	L	L	N	B
A	G	M	O	N	A	T	A	T	M	V	F	I	E	E
C	U	P	I	P	U	I	U	U	M	E	O	A	A	R
H	S	G	R	J	N	T	H	O	R	M	H	N	T	A
N	T	I	U	D	A	I	J	L	R	B	E	O	H	U
N	L	N	A	S	J	E	M	U	U	E	E	N	I	N
E	I	L	E	M	T	H	B	S	L	R	A	F	U	A
D	E	C	E	M	B	E	R	E	H	I	H	U	R	J

APRIL
____
____
____
____
JANUARY
______
______
______
MAY
______
NOVEMBER
OCTOBER
SEPTEMBER
______

______
AUGUST
KALENDER
DEZEMBER
FEBRUAR
____
JULI
JUNI
MÄRZ
______
MONAT
____
____
____
JAHR

REVIEW: TIME

65

Mix & Match: The translations in the word list below have been scrambled. Draw lines between the left and right hand columns to line up the matching words.

U	N	O	O	N	R	E	T	F	A	T	K	A	Ü	S
I	M	E	A	B	E	N	D	T	T	W	G	A	G	T
E	I	N	E	M	U	G	H	N	I	E	S	R	A	E
R	N	T	M	W	N	C	E	N	U	O	A	N	T	I
N	U	S	U	I	A	H	T	L	H	K	O	H	N	A
A	T	P	N	N	N	E	G	R	O	M	E	M	G	D
C	E	R	M	T	R	U	D	H	E	R	B	S	T	F
H	O	I	U	E	O	R	T	N	O	R	U	O	H	D
M	S	N	T	R	Ü	E	A	E	U	M	H	G	E	U
I	S	G	U	Y	V	M	N	E	M	T	S	A	T	A
T	E	E	A	E	W	M	O	E	Y	I	S	H	J	U
T	C	D	N	Ü	A	O	R	N	F	D	G	E	L	W
A	O	I	A	L	H	S	C	E	T	I	I	S	C	D
G	N	I	L	H	Ü	R	F	H	N	H	F	F	O	W
G	D	Y	L	T	E	D	W	E	E	K	C	Y	E	P

AFTERNOON	ABEND
AUTUMN	FRÜHLING
DAY	HERBST
EVENING	JAHR
HOUR	MINUTE
MINUTE	MONAT
MONTH	MORGEN
MORNING	NACHMITTAG
NIGHT	NACHT
SECOND	SEKUNDE
SPRING	SOMMER
SUMMER	STUNDE
WEEK	TAG
WINTER	WINTER
YEAR	WOCHE

REVIEW: COLOURS

66

Fill-in-the-Blanks: Find the missing translations hidden in the wordsearch grid and fill-in-the-blanks in the word list below. If you need some help, refer back to the original puzzle.

O	M	A	G	E	N	T	A	V	I	O	L	E	T	T
V	G	A	H	E	V	O	P	N	R	U	G	G	D	O
I	E	C	E	H	I	N	I	A	U	N	G	O	N	D
A	I	R	T	E	O	O	N	O	A	O	W	U	U	A
N	G	N	I	Y	L	G	K	R	R	U	T	O	A	D
E	N	E	H	C	E	E	O	E	G	O	Y	A	R	G
J	U	I	W	H	T	L	A	B	N	G	E	L	B	B
T	T	T	A	K	C	A	L	B	D	T	E	E	M	Y
H	O	U	H	W	V	U	I	O	K	B	U	A	M	E
R	H	N	T	H	E	N	U	ß	W	F	ß	R	D	E
W	E	Ü	I	H	Ü	T	A	I	I	L	O	T	E	B
T	H	H	N	R	O	C	L	Y	H	E	S	N	R	I
L	H	S	G	R	Y	R	B	C	Z	E	W	O	T	N
R	T	Ü	A	A	E	X	T	R	E	N	S	U	L	I
H	A	T	N	E	G	A	M	Z	R	A	W	H	C	S

BLACK ______________
BLUE _______
BROWN _________
CYAN ________
GRAY ________
GREEN ________
MAGENTA _____________
ORANGE ____________
PINK ________
RED ______
VIOLET ___________
WHITE _______
YELLOW _______

REVIEW: SHAPES

67

Fill-in-the-Blanks: Find the missing translations hidden in the wordsearch grid and fill-in-the-blanks in the word list below. If you need some help, refer back to the original puzzle.

E	L	G	N	A	T	C	E	R	A	U	Q	S	Y	X
D	K	C	E	S	H	C	E	S	S	O	K	A	I	O
E	I	P	X	E	R	C	N	T	S	H	C	L	N	V
D	T	Y	B	S	H	E	A	C	H	T	E	C	K	A
I	I	U	P	T	A	E	D	O	M	H	F	H	D	L
M	C	M	E	L	A	I	X	N	E	C	N	A	C	U
A	G	C	A	X	D	R	R	A	I	E	Ü	E	Y	T
R	K	U	I	R	L	U	D	D	G	L	F	H	L	R
Y	C	L	I	L	Y	N	T	A	E	O	Y	V	I	I
P	E	I	E	S	A	P	O	G	U	W	N	Z	N	A
H	I	G	R	A	G	V	U	G	Ü	Q	A	T	D	N
A	E	I	O	C	R	K	O	R	A	P	E	E	E	G
K	R	E	I	S	L	N	F	M	I	T	I	N	R	L
E	D	I	S	P	H	E	R	E	E	A	C	E	O	E
A	A	I	E	U	L	P	E	N	T	A	G	O	N	C

__________ ACHTECK
__________ DREIECK
__________ FÜNFECK
__________ HELIX
__________ KEGEL
__________ KREIS
__________ KUGEL
__________ OVAL
__________ PYRAMIDE
__________ QUADRAT
__________ RECHTECK
__________ SECHSECK
__________ WÜRFEL
__________ ZYLINDER

REVIEW: THE BODY

68

Fill-in-the-Blanks: Find the missing translations hidden in the wordsearch grid and fill-in-the-blanks in the word list below. If you need some help, refer back to the original puzzle.

E	K	N	E	L	E	G	D	N	A	H	H	A	T	T
L	I	F	R	T	R	U	G	M	T	I	I	R	E	I
H	E	I	T	A	O	U	G	U	W	A	P	M	P	P
Ö	A	G	A	S	N	U	O	N	H	R	P	U	A	M
H	N	H	I	I	I	M	T	D	O	L	I	L	A	R
L	I	W	L	N	E	A	I	E	E	T	M	S	Ä	A
E	N	R	L	L	B	E	W	S	O	L	O	E	T	E
S	H	Ö	E	O	C	K	R	Z	U	N	G	E	Ö	F
H	F	Ü	V	Ö	M	S	O	W	Ä	T	O	E	H	Ä
C	H	I	F	R	O	A	A	P	A	T	T	I	T	L
A	T	T	A	T	M	D	H	H	F	B	D	A	E	H
A	H	N	E	Ü	E	E	P	A	I	L	R	Z	E	C
I	A	D	Y	Ä	E	S	R	E	F	M	A	Y	E	S
R	T	N	E	L	R	A	T	S	A	U	M	C	P	H
N	O	F	E	A	E	H	C	Ä	L	F	D	N	A	H

ARM
______ CALF
______
______
______ HIP
______ MOUTH
PALM
______ TOE
______
______ WRIST

______ ACHSELHÖHLE
______ HAAR
KOPF
FERSE
______ BEIN
______
______ SCHLÄFE
______ ZUNGE
TAILLE
______

REVIEW: THE BODY 2

69

Mix & Match: The translations in the word list below have been scrambled. Draw lines between the left and right hand columns to line up the matching words.

W	N	E	R	B	R	U	S	T	W	A	R	Z	E	T
E	E	A	B	E	E	R	H	R	T	Y	E	P	K	S
D	L	T	A	T	A	A	O	S	H	A	G	A	O	C
A	A	L	I	E	N	A	U	N	N	O	N	S	E	H
L	E	U	B	D	W	R	L	G	O	A	I	T	B	U
B	R	R	M	O	B	H	D	H	E	S	F	R	ß	L
R	D	O	E	E	G	A	E	G	A	T	E	U	R	T
E	O	G	L	T	N	E	R	E	E	A	F	A	C	E
D	U	O	B	S	L	N	N	D	S	S	E	N	M	R
L	K	C	O	T	T	U	B	T	F	A	I	S	R	B
U	P	E	W	H	H	L	H	I	U	P	N	C	S	L
O	E	O	A	U	E	H	N	C	P	Ä	I	E	H	A
H	I	N	L	M	E	G	T	L	S	ß	F	O	O	T
S	D	ß	P	B	E	Y	E	G	E	S	Ä	ß	C	T
I	S	T	I	R	N	N	D	A	E	H	E	R	O	F

BREAST	AUGE
BUTTOCK	BRUST
EAR	BRUSTWARZE
ELBOW	DAUMEN
EYE	ELLBOGEN
FACE	FINGER
FINGER	FUß
FOOT	GESÄß
FOREHEAD	GESICHT
HAND	HAND
NIPPLE	NASE
NOSE	OHR
SHOULDER	SCHULTER
SHOULDER BLADE	SCHULTERBLATT
THUMB	STIRN

REVIEW: THE BODY 3

70

Fill-in-the-Blanks: Find the missing translations hidden in the wordsearch grid and fill-in-the-blanks in the word list below. If you need some help, refer back to the original puzzle.

L	E	G	A	N	R	E	G	N	I	F	H	O	E	O
K	Ö	R	P	E	R	C	R	R	T	H	Y	N	E	D
S	T	U	O	Ü	N	H	N	O	Ö	E	A	E	T	O
Y	R	P	E	R	H	E	I	M	C	B	O	D	Y	B
R	B	H	M	R	H	E	M	H	E	S	K	I	N	E
S	L	A	H	D	K	W	I	L	O	A	E	N	N	R
U	N	U	C	I	S	N	N	V	E	H	E	O	C	S
N	N	T	T	K	A	S	E	G	T	H	H	E	Z	C
T	I	L	T	V	E	A	N	E	H	E	C	T	Ä	H
E	S	N	E	L	N	A	E	K	I	N	N	Ö	H	E
R	E	L	C	K	W	T	C	N	G	E	Y	T	N	N
A	C	S	L	A	S	S	K	D	H	K	W	S	E	K
R	U	E	J	R	O	U	G	E	L	C	S	L	O	E
M	R	A	E	R	O	F	M	C	M	Ü	U	E	E	L
G	I	L	S	U	F	I	N	G	E	R	N	A	I	L

ANKLE ____________
BACK ____________
BODY ____________
CHEEK __________
CHIN ______
FINGERNAIL __________________
FOREARM ______________
KNEE ______
MUSCLES ____________
NAVEL ________
NECK _______
SKIN _______
TEETH ________
THIGH ____________________

REVIEW: THE BODY 4

71

Fill-in-the-Blanks: Find the missing translations hidden in the wordsearch grid and fill-in-the-blanks in the word list below. If you need some help, refer back to the original puzzle.

E	E	M	B	E	O	D	K	R	H	E	S	O	S	C
S	N	V	L	S	L	O	I	E	T	T	U	M	D	N
R	P	I	U	I	U	S	H	C	O	R	A	G	I	U
Y	E	R	T	R	N	K	P	M	K	L	M	A	S	R
E	W	C	R	S	G	N	A	L	L	D	R	E	E	S
N	A	A	T	H	E	C	E	I	E	B	A	G	S	O
D	Y	I	M	U	H	T	N	Y	S	E	D	R	M	E
I	A	Z	L	I	M	T	N	A	L	O	N	T	M	M
K	A	R	N	D	E	N	R	I	O	M	N	O	T	A
H	V	C	T	S	V	T	V	L	E	A	Ü	H	V	S
O	O	S	T	E	E	E	B	S	N	G	D	B	G	T
H	E	I	I	R	R	E	B	E	L	E	R	L	N	D
D	N	N	I	E	A	I	E	F	I	N	N	A	U	A
E	S	E	O	I	E	E	E	R	E	I	N	E	L	R
T	N	R	I	H	E	G	H	S	Z	R	E	H	V	M

__________ ARTERIEN
_______ BLUT
_______ _________ DICKDARM
_______ _________ DÜNNDARM
______ GEHIRN
______ HERZ
______ LEBER
______ LUNGE
_________ MAGEN
_______ MASTDARM
_______ MILZ
_______ NIERE
______ VENEN

REVIEW: LAND & SEA

72

Fill-in-the-Blanks: Find the missing translations hidden in the wordsearch grid and fill-in-the-blanks in the word list below. If you need some help, refer back to the original puzzle.

N E I S A N T A R C T I C A O
N A C I R F A N Ü E A P A E R
A C I T N A L T A K Y A I S E
E A K I R F A A I G E C S K E
N R S C H W A R Z E S I A C M
A C E I L S E K A T Ü F M A R
R T T V N M O T I O H I I L A
R I O O A D L I H F T C N B L
E C R D Z A I S O T I S D X O
T E Ü E N E O S E C R Z I F P
I S U T D U A L C U E O A Ü D
D Ü I R T S M N C H R A N P R
E K R H O E E H I E E O N L O
M P H Ü E P M A Ü E U R P I N
A K I R E M A D R O N G D E A

____
ARCTIC ocean
ASIA
________ ocean
BLACK SEA
EUROPE
INDIAN ocean
________ sea
NORTH america
OCEANIA
PACIFIC ocean
RED SEA
SOUTH america

AFRIKA
ANTARKTIS
____
ATLANTIK
________ meer
____
________ ozean
MITTELMEER
____
____
____
________ meer
____

REVIEW: WORLD MAP

73

Mix & Match: The translations in the word list below have been scrambled. Draw lines between the left and right hand columns to line up the matching words.

H	I	R	E	T	T	E	K	S	G	R	I	B	E	G
A	S	L	H	B	U	N	D	E	S	S	T	A	A	T
U	L	N	A	E	Z	O	C	O	U	N	T	R	Y	A
P	A	D	T	T	T	N	A	N	L	P	C	E	H	L
T	N	E	O	N	I	S	D	N	A	R	T	S	E	U
S	D	S	T	V	T	P	Ü	R	N	O	F	S	D	S
T	A	E	O	A	E	O	A	W	D	V	N	T	N	N
A	L	R	D	C	L	O	N	C	U	I	L	A	Y	I
D	P	T	P	F	R	P	U	A	B	N	Y	T	S	N
T	B	D	L	N	R	B	B	L	L	Z	I	E	C	E
N	S	U	A	E	N	T	A	E	S	C	K	L	R	P
O	ß	E	T	E	S	H	ß	E	E	A	Y	I	L	T
A	C	E	E	ß	P	N	D	E	L	E	V	F	R	A
O	H	C	A	E	B	E	I	R	E	E	M	S	A	E
D	M	O	U	N	T	A	I	N	R	A	N	G	E	D

BEACH	BUNDESSTAAT
CAPITAL	FLUß
CITY	GEBIRGSKETTE
COUNTRY	HALBINSEL
DESERT	HAUPTSTADT
ISLAND	INSEL
LAKE	LAND
MOUNTAIN RANGE	MEER
OCEAN	OZEAN
PENINSULA	PLATEAU
PLATEAU	PROVINZ
PROVINCE	SEE
RIVER	STADT
SEA	STRAND
STATE	WÜSTE

REVIEW: CITY MAP

Fill-in-the-Blanks: Find the missing translations hidden in the wordsearch grid and fill-in-the-blanks in the word list below. If you need some help, refer back to the original puzzle.

O	S	T	A	D	T	T	E	I	L	P	T	C	E	E
S	M	A	Y	S	P	G	C	O	I	R	I	E	T	K
T	O	E	H	A	D	M	O	N	U	M	E	N	T	C
N	T	F	R	I	E	D	H	O	F	V	K	Y	I	Ü
R	C	K	R	C	V	A	E	T	R	O	R	O	V	R
E	I	B	Y	R	B	A	G	N	D	B	A	T	U	B
B	R	V	C	N	B	N	H	A	K	S	P	L	G	O
O	T	N	E	S	D	A	O	L	T	M	D	N	S	U
U	S	S	M	R	B	R	H	R	E	F	A	T	O	L
L	I	A	E	O	L	R	A	N	E	H	R	L	M	E
E	D	C	T	I	V	ß	U	V	H	E	E	ß	A	V
V	F	U	A	Ü	E	R	T	B	E	O	L	U	H	A
A	A	R	R	W	G	R	A	T	U	N	F	L	D	R
R	Y	I	Y	A	W	H	G	I	H	S	U	F	A	D
D	R	A	I	L	R	O	A	D	L	I	N	E	H	E

AVENUE ______
BOULEVARD ______
BRIDGE ______
CEMETARY ______
DISTRICT ______
HIGHWAY ______
MONUMENT ______
PARK ______
RAILROAD LINE ______
RAILROAD station ______
RIVER ______
STREET ______
SUBURBS ______

REVIEW: WEATHER

75

Fill-in-the-Blanks: Find the missing translations hidden in the wordsearch grid and fill-in-the-blanks in the word list below. If you need some help, refer back to the original puzzle.

```
R F G E F R I E R E N D E R O
E I N F L U F T D R U C K A H
G E I M F T T T M N W I N D H
E R N T R A N R S C L O U D S
N U T B E R U T A R E P M E T
B A H N E E D D E I E T S D A
O R G T Z P N G R N N P Ö N R
G L I P I M N A A I R B R I K
E D L G N E F C K Ü Z A O W E
N W W A G T I R H I I Z A W R
E D A E U R A R O N R T L R R
K D R R R Q E M I S T R O E E
L O M U M G S B L I T Z U N G
O V H H E A V Y R A I N D H E
W Ö H N B A R O M E T R I C N
```

________	BLITZ
________	BÖ
____	DUNST
________ rain	GEFRIERENDER regen
________	HURRIKAN
________ pressure	LUFTDRUCK
______	RAUREIF
____	REGEN
________	REGENBOGEN
______	SPRÜHREGEN
______ ____	STARKER REGEN
____________	TEMPERATUR
_____	WARM
____	WIND
______	WOLKEN

REVIEW: WEATHER

76

Fill-in-the-Blanks: Find the missing translations hidden in the wordsearch grid and fill-in-the-blanks in the word list below. If you need some help, refer back to the original puzzle.

U S H E S O H R E S S A W O T
M R T L A K E H A I L D A H R
R W E D T R D H O N L A T L O
O E T T O R N A D O D A E I P
T S T S H L R H C N U I R G I
S C R T N U F I A T C S S H S
L H Y L I U N E F H H L P T C
A N W C T W D D T S A E O R H
C E O A L O E E E S Z B U A E
I E N O L O R G N R E E T I R
P R S M H R N N F N S N S N S
O E O A E P N E A O E T T F T
R G G G N S Y L E D G D O R U
T E E N H C S T N T O N I R R
L N D S W I R B E L S T U R M

_____

____

_____

FOG

HAIL

_____

_____ _____

SLEET

SNOW

THUNDERSTORM

____

TROPICAL STORM

____

____

KALT

WIRBELSTURM

TAU

______

______

DUNST

LEICHTER REGEN

____

____

____

TORNADO

_________ _____

TAIFUN

WASSERHOSE

REVIEW: ANIMALS 1

77

Mix & Match: The translations in the word list below have been scrambled. Draw lines between the left and right hand columns to line up the matching words.

G	R	O	U	N	D	H	O	G	Ö	W	D	D	L	C
N	E	A	Ö	R	I	H	O	Y	P	U	H	O	E	G
I	E	M	D	Y	U	U	R	F	W	A	I	N	E	E
E	M	U	E	N	E	S	E	L	R	O	I	K	O	N
W	A	L	D	M	U	R	M	E	L	T	I	E	R	T
H	U	E	A	S	D	L	E	M	A	C	P	Y	C	H
C	L	L	A	M	A	K	E	H	W	P	P	X	S	W
S	T	E	T	S	A	J	E	M	O	E	E	O	C	I
L	I	F	M	M	F	A	N	R	U	R	A	F	H	E
E	E	T	E	U	T	G	C	D	A	R	S	S	W	S
H	R	L	C	L	R	U	T	E	N	U	E	E	E	E
C	N	H	A	U	P	A	T	H	D	O	G	S	I	L
A	S	E	G	I	P	R	H	G	R	E	H	A	N	O
T	L	K	N	U	M	P	I	H	C	N	N	H	J	C
S	N	E	H	C	N	R	Ö	H	N	E	K	C	A	B

CAMEL
CHIPMUNK
DOG
DONKEY
FOX
GROUNDHOG
HARE
HORSE
JAGUAR
LEMUR
LLAMA
MULE
PIG
PORCUPINE
WEASEL

BACKENHÖRNCHEN
ESEL
FUCHS
HASE
HUND
JAGUAR
KAMEL
LAMA
LEMURE
MAULTIER
PFERD
SCHWEIN
STACHELSCHWEIN
WALDMURMELTIER
WIESEL

REVIEW: ANIMALS 2

Fill-in-the-Blanks: Find the missing translations hidden in the wordsearch grid and fill-in-the-blanks in the word list below. If you need some help, refer back to the original puzzle.

N	R	E	E	R	H	I	N	O	C	E	R	O	S	E
U	E	S	Ü	T	A	H	S	Ü	H	K	Ä	U	L	W
T	F	H	U	G	O	L	A	F	F	U	B	C	E	I
Y	N	C	N	O	O	B	A	B	H	S	H	R	N	L
W	G	O	H	H	B	K	Ü	A	T	A	C	A	A	D
I	E	A	R	E	L	I	M	F	M	E	S	B	I	B
L	P	N	L	G	E	S	R	S	F	H	A	B	V	O
D	A	O	Ü	D	T	T	T	A	O	E	W	I	A	A
S	R	G	O	E	R	E	A	R	C	B	L	T	P	R
C	D	A	R	H	R	A	N	H	I	C	C	R	G	U
H	B	Y	P	A	M	U	P	S	L	I	O	R	A	B
W	Ä	I	X	O	E	S	O	O	M	E	U	O	P	I
E	E	B	S	R	E	N	T	I	E	R	G	S	N	A
I	O	V	I	O	E	L	H	R	N	L	A	I	N	R
N	N	E	H	C	N	I	N	A	K	R	R	M	W	T

BABOON ________
BISON ________
BUFFALO ________
CARIBOU ________
CHEETAH ________
COUGAR ________
HAMSTER ________
HEDGEHOG ________
LEOPARD ________
MOOSE ________
OX ________
RABBIT ________
RACCOON ________
RHINOCEROS ________
WILD BOAR ________

REVIEW: ANIMALS 3

Fill-in-the-Blanks: Find the missing translations hidden in the wordsearch grid and fill-in-the-blanks in the word list below. If you need some help, refer back to the original puzzle.

B	L	H	I	P	P	O	P	O	T	A	M	U	S	E
S	O	E	T	T	A	R	P	G	I	R	A	F	F	E
U	O	H	L	T	T	A	S	O	A	C	I	T	Y	Z
A	R	E	I	T	K	N	I	T	S	R	E	P	B	N
M	A	I	V	L	P	G	E	K	G	S	A	N	A	A
R	G	W	E	H	Ö	U	S	I	Ä	D	U	T	L	P
E	N	A	D	C	F	T	R	O	R	N	U	M	L	M
D	A	L	N	E	T	A	A	E	P	G	G	O	A	I
E	K	L	L	T	F	N	F	L	N	O	E	U	W	H
L	N	A	E	F	E	P	A	A	L	R	S	T	R	C
F	U	B	E	W	L	L	R	F	H	I	O	S	H	U
D	K	Y	B	I	Ö	O	O	P	E	L	R	U	U	D
E	S	A	N	T	I	L	O	P	E	L	I	O	A	M
R	T	N	A	H	P	E	L	E	E	A	E	O	G	A
S	C	H	I	M	P	A	N	S	E	E	T	Ä	N	F

________	ANTILOPE
________	ELEFANT
___	FLEDERMAUS
______	GIRAFFE
______	GORILLA
________	KÄNGURU
___	LÖWE
____________	NILPFERD
_______	OPOSSUM
_________	ORANG-UTAN
___	RATTE
_________	SCHIMPANSE
____	STINKTIER
tasmanian _____	tasmanischer TEUFEL
_____	WALLABY

REVIEW: ANIMALS 4

Fill-in-the-Blanks: Find the missing translations hidden in the wordsearch grid and fill-in-the-blanks in the word list below. If you need some help, refer back to the original puzzle.

M B I B E R G I P A E N I U G
E N F M E S A R B E Z T Ö E A
E D R T A S U A M T T C Y B E
R L A N M O S O T S A C E I I
S Ä E C H N R H M R K A S W C
C Y B R H T I G E R V B O R H
H M R Z R S S G E E Ä C A T H
W Ä A E R I D T R R P N I G Ö
E Y L B R A U W A A U G T N R
I R O R B G W Q G S E B T A N
N Z P A Ä O O H S R B A N H C
C I O R L A L S C H A F A N H
H E T F H T F I A S U E I E E
E G T E N Ä Y H E H E K A M N
N E R A E B K C A L B S W U W

BADGER
BEAVER
______ _____
_____
MOUSE
GOAT
______ __
HYENA
POLAR BEAR
SHEEP
SQUIRREL
TIGER
WOLF
ZEBRA

____
SCHWARZBÄR
KATZE
KUH
______
MEERSCHWEINCHEN
____
____
____
____
______
______
____

REVIEW: BIRDS

81

Mix & Match: The translations in the word list below have been scrambled. Draw lines between the left and right hand columns to line up the matching words.

D	I	S	R	T	I	T	A	A	D	L	E	R	N	S
R	Y	E	K	R	U	T	E	E	E	S	O	O	G	S
I	W	T	Y	C	L	S	P	L	E	T	E	N	P	O
B	E	R	H	S	U	E	N	I	U	G	N	I	P	R
G	A	U	H	C	L	D	F	E	I	T	R	E	H	T
N	I	T	V	I	E	L	N	P	E	B	O	S	R	A
I	Y	H	C	U	A	P	S	I	I	B	O	W	N	B
M	R	A	E	M	L	N	S	L	U	R	U	R	L	L
M	N	H	I	U	A	T	O	T	T	G	A	A	T	A
U	S	N	O	G	L	K	U	A	R	B	N	V	T	A
H	G	E	T	O	U	E	B	R	E	A	O	E	M	A
O	G	N	I	M	A	L	F	L	E	L	U	N	P	T
P	E	L	I	K	A	N	G	S	E	O	I	ß	L	T
T	Y	L	E	D	E	A	H	C	I	R	T	S	O	H
W	O	O	D	P	E	C	K	E	R	E	I	E	G	H

ALBATROSS	ADLER
DUCK	ALBATROS
EAGLE	ENTE
FLAMINGO	EULE
GOOSE	FLAMINGO
HUMMINGBIRD	GANS
OSTRICH	GEIER
OWL	KOLIBRI
PELICAN	PELIKAN
PENGUIN	PINGUIN
PIGEON	RABE
RAVEN	SPECHT
TURKEY	STRAUß
VULTURE	TAUBE
WOODPECKER	TRUTHAHN

REVIEW: UNDER THE SEA

Fill-in-the-Blanks: Find the missing translations hidden in the wordsearch grid and fill-in-the-blanks in the word list below. If you need some help, refer back to the original puzzle.

L	H	D	R	T	I	N	T	E	N	F	I	S	C	H
A	E	A	N	H	F	Ü	S	E	A	L	H	D	R	C
W	O	G	I	U	M	I	N	R	E	T	S	E	E	S
T	L	A	I	M	H	E	S	G	R	U	I	L	A	H
R	T	A	L	E	W	E	Ö	C	P	E	F	P	O	U
E	N	E	W	Ö	E	O	E	O	H	L	R	H	T	S
W	R	A	L	ß	L	S	T	S	I	A	A	I	W	E
H	R	E	R	A	I	C	D	E	A	H	T	N	A	A
C	E	S	W	W	O	E	S	A	L	W	S	O	L	U
S	M	E	E	H	H	I	W	U	G	A	S	E	R	R
S	M	A	A	N	O	A	H	O	R	U	W	Y	O	C
H	U	L	I	P	H	A	L	I	E	L	L	R	ß	H
A	H	I	R	E	T	S	B	O	L	D	A	E	A	I
R	D	O	L	P	H	I	N	H	S	I	F	W	B	N
K	P	N	E	K	I	L	L	E	R	W	H	A	L	E

BELUGA ____________
DOLPHIN ____________
FISH ________
KILLER WHALE ___________________
LOBSTER ____________
NARWHAL ____________
OCTOPUS _________________
PORPOISE _____________
SEA LION _____________
SEA URCHIN ____________
SEAL _____________
SHARK _____
STARFISH ______________
WALRUS ____________
WHALE ______

REVIEW: INSECTS

83

Fill-in-the-Blanks: Find the missing translations hidden in the wordsearch grid and fill-in-the-blanks in the word list below. If you need some help, refer back to the original puzzle.

E	A	H	H	H	O	N	I	G	B	I	E	N	E	T
S	T	Z	O	A	H	O	N	E	Y	B	E	E	Y	E
C	N	I	H	R	A	M	E	I	S	E	B	L	E	K
H	L	K	M	I	N	H	O	R	S	E	F	L	Y	C
M	E	A	A	R	R	E	O	O	L	R	A	U	C	A
E	M	D	D	F	E	T	T	B	E	U	E	N	O	J
T	M	E	L	Y	I	T	M	T	S	L	T	T	D	W
T	U	O	L	K	B	U	T	H	I	O	I	N	R	O
E	H	F	S	Y	B	U	O	E	A	U	M	A	A	L
R	F	O	I	E	B	R	G	E	Q	S	R	A	G	L
L	M	L	R	I	N	L	E	S	R	E	E	D	O	E
I	E	E	I	I	A	P	O	M	K	H	T	A	N	Y
N	E	P	S	E	W	M	A	E	S	T	G	C	F	N
G	T	S	L	T	G	L	E	L	L	E	B	I	L	E
R	E	F	Ä	K	N	E	I	R	A	M	N	C	Y	A

_____ AMEISE
_____ BREMSE
_____ FLIEGE
_____ FLOH
_____ HONIGBIENE
_____ HORNISSE
_____ HUMMEL
_____ LAUS
_____ LIBELLE
_____ MARIENKÄFER
_____ MOSKITO
_____ SCHMETTERLING
_____ TERMITE
_____ WESPE
_____ ZIKADE

REVIEW: REPTILES & AMPHIBIANS

Fill-in-the-Blanks: Find the missing translations hidden in the wordsearch grid and fill-in-the-blanks in the word list below. If you need some help, refer back to the original puzzle.

K	L	A	P	P	E	R	S	C	H	L	A	N	G	E
U	I	L	N	O	E	L	Ä	M	A	H	C	T	E	A
Ä	D	L	T	A	L	L	I	G	A	T	O	R	N	J
E	O	I	E	W	R	C	I	E	O	A	U	A	O	E
E	K	G	L	A	S	H	S	D	D	E	U	V	H	K
T	O	A	S	O	I	A	A	O	O	G	E	I	T	A
Ö	R	T	N	C	C	M	L	F	I	C	R	P	Y	N
R	K	O	E	S	H	E	A	A	R	C	O	E	P	S
K	F	R	O	G	R	L	M	N	M	O	N	R	A	E
D	L	Ö	Ö	H	S	E	A	N	A	A	S	O	C	L
L	I	P	Y	T	H	O	N	N	U	R	N	C	R	T
I	Z	D	M	S	E	N	D	G	G	N	A	D	H	T
H	A	T	E	S	H	C	E	D	I	E	Y	W	E	A
C	R	E	P	I	V	L	R	E	L	T	R	U	T	R
S	D	R	A	Z	I	L	R	O	T	I	N	O	M	A

____
____
____
_____
______
LIZARD

________ _______
____
RATTLESNAKE
SALAMANDER

______
TOAD
TURTLE

______

ALLIGATOR
CHAMÄLEON
KROKODIL
FROSCH
LEGUAN

____
WARAN
PYTHON

____

____
SCHLANGE

______

____
VIPER

REVIEW: LIFE

85

Mix & Match: The translations in the word list below have been scrambled. Draw lines between the left and right hand columns to line up the matching words.

N	R	T	S	D	I	N	H	C	A	R	A	A	A	P
T	E	E	S	Ä	Ä	N	H	N	E	B	M	A	F	K
Ä	E	R	S	D	U	S	E	P	R	P	E	L	P	C
G	R	E	O	S	R	G	T	I	H	S	A	G	R	A
E	E	I	H	T	E	I	E	I	L	N	S	E	I	R
R	I	T	F	C	L	R	B	T	Z	I	I	N	M	N
O	T	E	I	E	S	I	F	E	I	N	T	A	A	I
D	L	G	S	S	A	I	N	H	S	E	L	P	T	V
E	E	A	H	N	I	F	F	E	C	G	R	T	E	O
N	T	N	S	I	R	E	K	Ä	A	S	E	E	S	R
T	U	E	R	E	I	T	N	E	N	N	I	P	S	E
S	E	G	S	H	E	R	B	I	V	O	R	E	S	S
E	B	S	U	N	M	A	R	S	U	P	I	A	L	S
N	E	T	A	M	I	R	P	I	L	E	G	Ö	V	F
R	N	E	I	B	I	H	P	M	A	M	M	A	L	S

ALGAE	ALGEN
AMPHIBIANS	AMPHIBIEN
ARACHNIDS	BEUTELTIERE
BIRDS	FISCHE
CARNIVORES	FLEISCHFRESSER
FISH	INSEKTEN
HERBIVORES	NAGETIERE
INSECTS	PFLANZENFRESSER
MAMMALS	PRIMATEN
MARSUPIALS	REPTILIEN
PRIMATES	SÄUGETIERE
REPTILES	SPINNENTIERE
RODENTS	VÖGEL

REVIEW: FAMILY

86

Fill-in-the-Blanks: Find the missing translations hidden in the wordsearch grid and fill-in-the-blanks in the word list below. If you need some help, refer back to the original puzzle.

L	E	A	Y	O	T	G	R	O	ß	V	A	T	E	R
W	M	H	L	I	E	L	T	E	R	N	R	H	H	E
E	C	E	I	N	T	W	N	R	D	T	I	B	E	H
P	F	A	M	I	L	I	E	T	E	N	O	N	F	T
G	A	D	A	U	E	H	R	H	O	T	I	U	F	A
R	R	R	F	U	T	D	D	L	P	C	A	K	E	F
A	E	E	E	A	N	Y	L	O	M	E	H	V	N	D
N	H	T	F	N	H	T	I	A	N	U	N	T	T	N
D	T	S	H	N	T	B	H	I	L	E	T	N	E	A
M	O	I	O	G	R	S	C	H	W	E	S	T	E	R
O	M	S	N	O	U	H	H	E	L	W	K	U	E	G
T	R	I	T	T	T	A	A	E	L	T	A	N	A	R
H	O	H	N	E	R	E	D	U	R	B	I	C	O	P
E	E	S	O	H	N	R	E	T	N	A	T	L	N	O
R	R	E	T	T	U	M	ß	O	R	G	K	E	A	E

AUNT ________
BROTHER ________
CHILDREN ________
DAUGHTER ________
FAMILY ________
FATHER ________
GRANDFATHER ________
GRANDMOTHER ________
MOTHER ________
NEPHEW ________
NIECE ________
PARENTS ________
SISTER ________
SON ________
UNCLE ________

REVIEW: FAMILY 2

87

Fill-in-the-Blanks: Find the missing translations hidden in the wordsearch grid and fill-in-the-blanks in the word list below. If you need some help, refer back to the original puzzle.

S	S	N	R	E	T	A	V	ß	O	R	G	R	U	S
U	G	C	W	E	N	N	A	M	E	H	E	A	C	S
O	R	A	H	T	N	H	C	G	O	T	C	H	E	T
N	E	G	G	W	U	K	A	H	H	T	W	N	S	N
B	A	T	R	S	I	W	E	G	I	I	H	C	U	E
N	T	C	B	O	H	E	U	L	E	L	H	E	A	R
O	E	A	O	C	ß	A	G	G	K	W	D	B	R	A
S	N	E	S	U	D	M	E	E	Ä	I	R	R	F	P
D	K	G	F	D	S	R	U	G	R	O	N	L	E	D
N	E	N	N	I	M	I	E	T	T	V	H	D	M	N
A	L	A	S	U	W	R	N	H	T	S	A	E	E	A
R	R	T	T	N	I	R	E	S	V	E	T	T	E	R
G	E	T	D	N	A	R	G	T	A	E	R	G	E	G
R	E	N	K	E	L	I	N	T	F	A	T	H	E	R
R	N	N	R	E	T	L	E	ß	O	R	G	R	U	A

__________ EHEMANN
__________ ENKEL
__________ ENKELIN
grand__________ ENKELKINDER
_____ FRAU
__________-in-law SCHWAGER
__________-in-law SCHWÄGERIN
__________-in-law SCHWIEGERMUTTER
__________-in-law SCHWIEGERVATER
great __________ URGROßELTERN
______ ______mother URGROßMUTTER
________grandfather URGROßVATER
________ VETTER

REVIEW: VERBS

88

Fill-in-the-Blanks: Find the missing translations hidden in the wordsearch grid and fill-in-the-blanks in the word list below. If you need some help, refer back to the original puzzle.

S	T	S	W	M	A	N	R	E	R	B	A	C	D	W
T	N	T	I	O	H	O	C	Y	F	E	C	H	E	O
O	E	T	O	W	A	I	T	O	R	L	Ö	A	E	L
C	G	H	N	A	W	H	L	O	R	R	A	E	Ä	L
H	N	K	N	D	S	G	A	D	E	A	A	S	E	O
A	I	O	K	E	E	K	A	N	U	A	E	C	Y	F
N	S	O	N	N	K	E	Ö	G	S	E	T	H	O	O
G	T	C	I	S	R	N	N	P	E	E	L	S	O	T
E	K	O	H	O	T	I	E	H	H	E	E	S	O	T
S	O	T	T	L	S	Ä	N	D	E	R	N	P	I	R
D	C	A	O	O	A	E	H	B	N	E	A	N	Ä	N
O	H	V	T	R	T	F	O	Ä	G	Y	D	E	R	I
N	E	G	A	R	T	T	E	A	E	I	T	S	T	E
D	N	A	A	T	I	I	R	N	E	S	S	E	U	S
A	U	W	L	B	E	F	B	E	Z	A	H	L	E	N

TO ASK

TO CHANGE
TO COOK

TO READ

TO SING

TO THINK
TO WAIT

SEIN
TRAGEN

ESSEN
FOLGEN
HÖREN
BEZAHLEN

SEHEN

SCHLAFEN

REVIEW: VERBS 2

89

Mix & Match: The translations in the word list below have been scrambled. Draw lines between the left and right hand columns to line up the matching words.

L	Y	D	H	N	T	O	L	O	O	K	F	O	R	N
I	ß	P	E	H	A	B	E	N	H	N	T	O	E	E
E	H	L	L	E	S	O	T	E	E	A	C	H	V	H
B	A	E	F	G	S	E	T	H	R	M	C	A	N	E
E	R	H	E	E	M	O	C	O	T	E	H	H	W	T
N	B	O	N	C	C	U	E	O	R	O	T	E	O	S
E	E	T	O	L	S	U	S	P	T	S	F	W	N	R
ß	I	F	O	N	E	P	S	T	O	D	O	I	N	E
E	T	S	U	D	E	C	P	T	E	R	E	E	N	V
I	E	F	O	A	R	S	R	E	K	Y	M	E	C	D
L	N	I	K	T	K	I	I	T	K	M	R	V	P	H
H	E	N	O	Y	N	R	N	E	O	A	A	O	L	I
C	T	D	T	K	R	U	E	K	R	F	T	L	B	N
S	E	E	E	A	T	L	E	V	A	R	T	O	T	O
O	D	N	A	T	S	R	E	D	N	U	O	T	T	G

TO CLOSE	ARBEITEN
TO COME	FINDEN
TO DO	HABEN
TO DRINK	HELFEN
TO FIND	KOMMEN
TO HAVE	LIEBEN
TO HELP	NEHMEN
TO LOOK FOR	REISEN
TO LOVE	SCHLIEßEN
TO SELL	SPRECHEN
TO SPEAK	SUCHEN
TO TAKE	TRINKEN
TO TRAVEL	TUN
TO UNDERSTAND	VERKAUFEN
TO WORK	VERSTEHEN

REVIEW: VERBS 3

90

Fill-in-the-Blanks: Find the missing translations hidden in the wordsearch grid and fill-in-the-blanks in the word list below. If you need some help, refer back to the original puzzle.

T	S	C	H	R	E	I	B	E	N	C	O	N	H	N
O	C	P	G	A	E	N	V	D	E	K	E	T	T	O
B	H	Y	I	B	T	A	E	S	Ö	Z	M	O	O	W
E	U	U	R	E	E	S	K	N	N	N	G	D	O	T
A	L	B	T	L	L	L	N	A	F	O	E	N	W	G
B	D	O	O	B	A	E	T	A	A	F	K	H	E	E
L	E	T	I	W	N	W	N	N	Y	O	Ö	B	E	O
E	N	T	O	A	T	I	M	E	T	A	E	R	T	G
T	C	T	O	O	E	S	X	L	N	N	L	E	D	R
O	U	N	G	R	P	S	E	L	K	R	N	P	T	E
R	Y	I	A	N	U	E	L	O	A	N	E	S	O	R
F	V	R	O	D	A	N	N	W	U	S	E	L	T	T
E	T	I	R	W	O	T	H	E	F	A	R	H	I	T
N	E	N	N	E	R	T	O	L	E	A	R	N	E	T
A	B	F	A	H	R	E	N	T	N	A	W	O	T	G

TO BE ABLE TO ________
TO BUY ________
TO DANCE ________
TO GIVE ________
TO GO ________
TO KNOW ________
TO LEARN ________
TO LEAVE ________
TO OPEN ________
TO OWE ________
TO PLAY ________
TO RUN ________
TO WALK ________
TO WANT ________
TO WRITE ________

REVIEW: FOOD

91

Fill-in-the-Blanks: Find the missing translations hidden in the wordsearch grid and fill-in-the-blanks in the word list below. If you need some help, refer back to the original puzzle.

R	A	G	U	S	N	W	O	R	B	Z	M	W	B	L
S	O	I	H	E	S	G	G	E	U	P	A	I	E	R
E	T	H	C	Ü	R	F	S	C	A	M	S	E	L	E
L	R	E	L	N	A	Ü	K	S	E	E	S	H	N	K
B	S	D	I	E	M	E	T	A	L	O	C	O	H	C
A	R	C	M	E	R	A	T	O	O	S	B	P	E	U
T	E	I	G	W	A	R	E	N	I	A	L	Ä	G	Z
E	T	E	L	K	R	F	R	E	T	T	U	B	I	R
G	T	D	F	C	A	K	L	A	R	H	O	E	N	E
E	U	E	L	F	Ä	F	E	O	N	O	D	Y	O	N
V	B	H	E	S	O	R	F	R	U	I	T	E	H	U
E	E	S	E	E	H	C	A	E	E	R	E	N	K	A
M	S	C	T	O	N	I	W	G	E	I	H	O	E	R
T	E	N	A	P	Ü	L	Ä	Ä	U	R	E	H	T	B
S	C	H	O	K	O	L	A	D	E	S	H	R	Ä	N

______ ______ BRAUNER ZUCKER
______ BUTTER
______ EIER
______ FLEISCH
______ FRÜCHTE
______ GEMÜSE
______ HONIG
______ KAFFEE
______ KÄSE
______ MEHL
______ MILCH
______ SCHOKOLADE
______ TEE
______ TEIGWAREN
______ ZUCKER

REVIEW: FOOD 2

92

Fill-in-the-Blanks: Find the missing translations hidden in the wordsearch grid and fill-in-the-blanks in the word list below. If you need some help, refer back to the original puzzle.

H	C	S	I	E	L	F	E	N	I	E	W	H	C	S
R	T	A	I	R	Ö	T	P	P	A	E	C	I	U	E
E	E	F	R	I	C	E	O	S	F	S	R	A	R	N
N	B	T	N	R	P	R	A	N	I	E	T	I	E	I
I	E	R	R	P	K	L	M	E	S	R	F	T	I	R
R	B	E	E	R	T	U	L	S	E	E	A	F	B	A
A	G	R	T	A	B	F	A	I	H	H	H	S	E	G
G	A	A	A	T	D	W	S	T	E	A	K	O	E	R
R	I	S	W	N	E	K	C	I	H	C	O	Y	F	A
A	E	I	I	H	D	S	A	L	Z	F	I	Ö	R	M
M	M	R	I	U	P	S	C	K	A	B	L	U	E	E
K	E	R	A	H	F	W	S	T	A	M	I	I	J	T
Ö	N	D	D	T	Y	T	T	F	P	E	B	R	O	T
T	A	C	E	K	L	E	W	K	N	E	T	E	H	W
P	L	T	F	L	A	M	M	F	L	E	I	S	C	H

BEEF
BEER
____
____
JUICE
LAMB
MARGARINE
____
PEPPER
____
RICE
SALT
____
____

____
____
BROT
HUHN
____
____
____
ÖL
____
SCHWEINEFLEISCH
____
____
STEAK
WASSER

REVIEW: FOOD 3

93

Mix & Match: The translations in the word list below have been scrambled. Draw lines between the left and right hand columns to line up the matching words.

W	E	N	H	A	S	E	R	U	A	S	L	A	E	V
S	R	A	I	A	Y	O	G	U	R	T	C	O	G	N
R	W	T	N	E	O	N	U	E	A	D	U	C	K	O
M	S	A	P	H	W	W	T	R	U	H	G	O	J	O
O	L	N	S	O	I	N	U	U	C	A	A	C	N	A
M	N	I	A	N	E	Y	L	C	R	R	S	G	S	H
A	I	L	E	G	N	I	R	K	T	K	E	N	C	O
P	L	E	S	T	T	I	E	T	I	F	E	A	S	R
L	K	C	Ü	I	L	N	R	M	L	H	S	Y	M	N
E	A	I	B	A	T	E	E	Ü	C	U	O	P	M	S
S	K	B	I	W	T	L	G	N	M	F	O	D	E	I
Y	A	V	L	U	A	E	I	A	H	A	G	P	O	R
R	O	O	P	S	L	N	Y	E	B	A	E	D	B	U
U	S	E	S	S	A	L	O	M	O	H	S	R	I	P
P	O	E	M	K	A	L	B	F	L	E	I	S	C	H

BAGEL	AHORNSIRUP
COCOA	ENTE
CREAM	GANS
DUCK	GEFLÜGEL
GOOSE	JOGHURT
MAPLE SYRUP	KAKAO
MOLASSES	KALBFLEISCH
POULTRY	KANINCHEN
RABBIT	KRINGEL
SOUR CREAM	MELASSE
TURKEY	PUTER
VEAL	SAHNE
YOGURT	SAURE SAHNE
WINE	WEIN

REVIEW: FRUITS

94

Fill-in-the-Blanks: Find the missing translations hidden in the wordsearch grid and fill-in-the-blanks in the word list below. If you need some help, refer back to the original puzzle.

N	N	E	R	E	E	B	L	E	D	I	E	H	N	W
P	E	A	C	H	W	V	O	A	G	P	A	P	E	A
S	M	C	U	G	R	A	P	E	F	R	U	I	T	S
T	U	S	E	N	O	R	T	I	Z	A	N	N	T	S
R	A	L	R	O	I	O	R	E	V	T	O	E	E	E
A	L	L	P	K	O	S	R	A	R	M	E	A	M	R
W	F	T	O	C	I	R	P	A	E	M	N	P	I	M
B	P	S	P	C	O	S	U	L	N	P	E	P	L	E
E	E	S	H	R	E	B	T	O	R	G	A	L	T	L
R	G	R	A	P	E	F	R	U	I	T	E	E	O	O
R	R	N	A	N	E	R	E	E	B	D	R	E	K	N
I	G	R	U	L	A	A	U	B	E	R	G	I	N	E
E	G	G	P	L	A	N	T	U	M	N	K	O	E	K
S	M	U	L	P	A	E	A	E	I	I	V	B	W	H
S	E	I	R	R	E	B	E	U	L	B	O	T	D	D

APRICOT ____________
BLUEBERRIES ____________
EGGPLANT ____________
GRAPEFRUIT ____________
GRAPES ____________
LEMON ____________
LIME ____________
ORANGE ____________
PEACH ____________
PEAR ____________
PINEAPPLE ____________
PLUMS ____________
STRAWBERRIES ____________
WATERMELON ____________

REVIEW: FRUITS 2

Fill-in-the-Blanks: Find the missing translations hidden in the wordsearch grid and fill-in-the-blanks in the word list below. If you need some help, refer back to the original puzzle.

S N B R O N D O N E N Y S R R
E C A E O A E I T E A E R E A
I T N T N S K R R A I L B B K
R R A A N P T E E R M L N M I
R R N N M E E O R E E O G U R
E A E U A B H E M G B W T C P
B K P L M R H C E A R M B U A
K Ü F O P C G O S G T O I C P
C R R A S P B E R R I E S H R
A B L E F P A F M S I E O O E
L I N I H C C U Z O O K F O N
B S F G R A N A T A P F E L Ü
I O D I C N E R S D R E T O R
O E T O G A Z U C C H I N I G
R E P P E P N E E R G U R K E

______	APFEL
______	BANANE
__________	BROMBEEREN
___	FEIGE
______ pepper	GELBER paprika
__________	GRANATAPFEL
______ ______	GRÜNER PAPRIKA
________	GURKE
__________	HIMBEEREN
_______	KIRSCHEN
______	KÜRBIS
___ pepper	ROTER paprika
______	TOMATE
_______	ZUCCHINI

REVIEW: VEGETABLES

96

Fill-in-the-Blanks: Find the missing translations hidden in the wordsearch grid and fill-in-the-blanks in the word list below. If you need some help, refer back to the original puzzle.

G	R	L	F	B	L	U	M	E	N	K	O	H	L	M
B	Y	A	I	E	T	U	A	G	A	B	A	T	U	R
S	O	U	D	N	N	B	B	R	O	C	C	O	L	I
H	H	C	M	I	E	C	T	O	M	L	R	G	ß	A
C	C	H	A	A	E	I	H	F	L	E	A	A	T	R
A	K	R	N	D	C	S	O	E	D	E	D	R	E	T
U	O	N	G	H	M	T	C	H	L	K	I	L	E	I
L	B	T	O	Ü	D	R	A	H	C	S	S	I	W	S
I	L	K	L	B	S	O	O	N	E	K	H	C	S	C
F	E	P	D	A	L	K	N	T	I	N	A	D	E	H
L	N	S	P	I	N	A	C	H	T	P	A	P	N	O
O	N	S	L	E	S	S	U	R	B	S	S	H	H	C
W	E	L	S	H	I	L	O	C	C	O	R	B	O	K
E	F	O	B	E	E	S	K	O	H	L	R	Ü	B	E
R	R	T	S	Ü	ß	K	A	R	T	O	F	F	E	L

____________ ARTISCHOCKE
____ ______ PAK-CHOI
____________ BROCCOLI
BRUSSELS sprouts ____________
CAULIFLOWER ____________
____________ FENCHEL
GARLIC ____________
green BEAN grüne ____________
____________ LAUCH
RADISH ____________
____________ KOHLRÜBE
____________ SPINAT
________ potato SÜßKARTOFFEL
SWISS CHARD ____________

REVIEW: VEGETABLES 2

97

Mix & Match: The translations in the word list below have been scrambled. Draw lines between the left and right hand columns to line up the matching words.

```
T P R N Y P F E C A B B A G E
A I L O L K A R O T T E T I D
L N C E L E T S L T O R R A C
A S E A B E F E T E N E H N N
S R L S E E G F A I L S V E G
P A E B B R I S O L N E R S A
O P R T A R P W E T G A A B S
T N Y P E A E S Z E R E K R C
A T S E R E N R T L P A O E H
T Ü U A C E B A E W H N K E A
O Ü G R G U B E O K I O S N L
E U E N N L T N T O C Ü K Ü O
S T A P E I S T N O M U H R T
T T A S A E P N E E R G Z G T
S H A L L O T I G L R Ü B E E
```

ASPARAGUS	GEMÜSE
BEET	GRÜNE ERBSEN
CABBAGE	KAROTTE
CARROT	KARTOFFELN
CELERY	KOHL
GREEN PEAS	PASTINAKE
LETTUCE	ROTE BEETE
ONION	RÜBE
PARSNIP	SALAT
POTATOES	SCHALOTTE
SHALLOT	SPARGEL
SNOW PEAS	STANGENSELLERIE
TURNIP	ZUCKERERBSEN
VEGETABLES	ZWIEBEL

REVIEW: SEAFOOD

98

Fill-in-the-Blanks: Find the missing translations hidden in the wordsearch grid and fill-in-the-blanks in the word list below. If you need some help, refer back to the original puzzle.

L	H	C	S	I	F	N	U	H	T	T	R	U	S	E
E	A	T	K	R	A	K	E	U	U	D	P	H	T	V
H	O	A	T	N	Y	G	N	L	I	E	C	U	N	E
C	L	A	M	S	V	A	A	U	L	A	X	M	K	N
S	C	A	L	L	O	P	Q	R	L	E	A	M	O	U
U	P	M	I	R	H	S	D	S	N	Y	D	E	O	S
M	T	C	A	L	C	T	K	M	C	E	E	R	U	M
M	N	M	C	T	N	R	U	O	R	H	L	P	A	U
M	E	U	R	C	A	S	Y	B	O	T	O	E	K	S
A	Y	S	A	B	C	S	U	A	I	T	R	L	A	C
K	N	S	B	H	T	H	U	E	C	L	E	E	L	H
D	W	E	E	E	E	S	N	O	M	L	A	S	M	E
D	D	L	R	L	T	T	U	B	I	L	A	H	A	L
E	N	S	E	E	O	L	O	B	S	T	E	R	R	N
T	Y	T	R	G	E	S	H	A	T	I	M	E	S	E

ANCHOVY __________
CLAMS ________________
CRAB ________
EEL ____
HALIBUT _________
LOBSTER ________
MUSSELS __________
OCTOPUS _______
OYSTERS ________
SALMON _______
SCALLOP ______________
SHRIMP _________
SOLE _________
SQUID ________
TUNA __________

REVIEW: HERBS

99

Fill-in-the-Blanks: Find the missing translations hidden in the wordsearch grid and fill-in-the-blanks in the word list below. If you need some help, refer back to the original puzzle.

B	A	S	I	L	I	K	U	M	E	E	C	S	E	F
A	H	B	C	H	E	E	I	E	O	U	T	Y	O	H
I	O	R	M	L	M	N	G	A	Y	Z	T	O	I	R
E	N	E	E	Y	Z	A	R	E	T	U	Ä	R	K	T
E	S	H	H	E	S	A	L	B	E	I	T	I	P	B
C	W	T	R	H	B	S	A	V	O	R	Y	G	E	O
O	E	I	R	N	R	R	O	N	D	Y	O	A	I	H
R	E	D	N	A	I	R	O	K	I	T	R	N	M	N
I	T	R	P	I	G	D	I	L	T	S	E	O	O	E
A	B	D	A	M	R	O	I	O	E	T	G	G	Ä	N
N	A	T	N	Y	I	A	N	L	I	S	A	B	U	K
D	Y	H	I	H	E	N	M	H	L	R	N	E	A	R
E	E	A	S	T	W	Ä	T	S	R	I	O	O	I	A
R	O	S	E	M	A	R	Y	A	O	E	D	E	F	U
E	I	L	I	S	R	E	T	E	P	R	H	T	I	T

_____ ANIS
_____ BASILIKUM
_____ BOHNENKRAUT
_____ DILL
_____ ESTRAGON
_____ KORIANDER
_____ KRÄUTER
_____ _____ LORBEER
_____ MINZE
_____ ORIGANO
_____ PETERSILIE
_____ ROSMARIN
_____ SALBEI
_____ THYMIAN

REVIEW: HOUSE

100

Fill-in-the-Blanks: Find the missing translations hidden in the wordsearch grid and fill-in-the-blanks in the word list below. If you need some help, refer back to the original puzzle.

I L R E M M I Z F A L H C S E
R A W S H M O O R D E B D B G
L O K I T C H E N O K L A B A
Z I I T N O Ü H G D R T C R R
M U B E D D O K R A H I H E A
O R F A G U O I H R R C W M G
O E L A S L V W O C O A O M Y
R M A E R E E O R I S O G I N
G M W L W H M E F A R A E Z O
N I N A C T T E B G S K W S C
I Z Y Ü N S B S N C B E T S L
N N K Ü N H U I W T T L N E A
I H V E Ü A V R E E E L L A B
D O F O H I F O O R G E N E H
C W R A L A U N D R Y R O O M

BALCONY
______
BATHROOM
______
BEDROOM
DINING ROOM
______
______
HOUSE
______
LAUNDRY ROOM
LAWN
______ ______
______
WINDOW

______
KELLER
______
BETT
______
______
ZUFARHTSWEG
GARAGE
______
KÜCHE
______
______
WOHNZIMMER
DACH
______

REVIEW: HOUSE 2

101

Mix & Match: The translations in the word list below have been scrambled. Draw lines between the left and right hand columns to line up the matching words.

B	A	T	H	T	U	B	A	V	W	R	T	H	K	C
S	E	L	B	A	T	U	O	F	B	D	Z	O	U	E
C	O	L	O	O	P	R	I	L	R	A	M	R	G	N
H	S	F	I	V	H	R	U	E	U	M	T	L	U	I
W	C	O	A	A	E	B	S	N	O	A	Ü	Z	A	H
I	W	G	N	P	T	S	E	D	I	H	E	W	B	C
M	W	G	L	H	E	T	E	N	L	H	D	E	R	S
M	C	A	G	R	A	H	E	A	O	N	E	I	O	A
B	C	I	S	D	L	H	M	C	T	I	C	S	V	M
E	L	N	T	H	E	P	R	A	U	M	N	I	H	H
C	H	A	N	D	E	L	I	E	R	A	E	T	C	C
K	A	A	S	P	O	R	C	H	S	K	F	Z	S	S
E	N	N	A	W	E	D	A	B	Ü	S	R	E	I	A
N	D	T	E	B	A	A	F	O	S	N	A	R	T	W
K	R	O	N	L	E	U	C	H	T	E	R	W	T	O

BATHTUB	BADEWANNE
CHANDELIER	GLÜHLAMPE
CURTAIN	KAMIN
DRESSER	KOMMODE
FAUCET	KRONLEUCHTER
FENCE	SCHWIMMBECKEN
FIREPLACE	SOFA
LIGHT BULB	TISCH
LOVESEAT	VORBAU
POOL	VORHANG
PORCH	WASCHMASCHINE
SOFA	WASSERHAHN
TABLE	ZAUN
WASHER	ZWEISITZER

REVIEW: HOUSE 3

Fill-in-the-Blanks: Find the missing translations hidden in the wordsearch grid and fill-in-the-blanks in the word list below. If you need some help, refer back to the original puzzle.

K	L	R	O	T	A	R	E	G	I	R	F	E	R	H
L	U	Y	S	T	A	I	R	S	R	O	R	R	I	M
E	H	E	D	E	Ü	E	I	A	H	W	E	G	H	T
I	N	U	M	I	W	N	R	A	A	H	H	A	O	R
D	G	A	T	O	K	M	L	S	E	C	C	R	C	E
E	I	L	H	S	C	L	C	W	H	S	S	D	H	P
R	T	S	E	H	N	H	E	A	D	I	U	E	S	P
S	T	E	A	G	B	H	I	L	A	T	D	R	T	E
C	E	I	D	E	E	R	E	R	E	B	E	O	U	C
H	R	A	C	I	B	I	M	L	T	I	S	B	H	L
R	B	K	N	I	B	O	P	I	M	E	D	E	L	O
A	E	O	D	N	I	E	T	S	N	R	O	H	C	S
N	T	E	N	R	O	S	H	S	I	H	A	D	I	E
K	T	Y	E	N	M	I	H	C	T	C	R	I	B	T
D	D	E	S	K	N	A	R	H	C	S	L	H	Ü	K

ARMCHAIR ____________________
ARMOIRE ______________________
BIDET _______
CHIMNEY __________________
CLOSET ________________
CRIB ________________
DESK __________________
HALL _______
HIGH CHAIR ________________
MIRROR ___________
REFRIGERATOR ___________________
SHOWER ___________
SINK ___________________
STAIRS __________

REVIEW: AT THE TABLE

103

Fill-in-the-Blanks: Find the missing translations hidden in the wordsearch grid and fill-in-the-blanks in the word list below. If you need some help, refer back to the original puzzle.

Y	R	E	U	E	R	T	S	R	E	F	F	E	F	P
O	K	P	E	T	T	E	I	V	R	E	S	S	R	S
S	A	L	G	N	C	R	H	E	A	O	P	T	A	N
E	E	A	M	T	E	L	L	C	D	H	O	E	G	K
N	T	T	R	P	E	L	E	R	T	G	O	A	U	T
N	S	E	P	E	E	W	E	F	U	I	N	K	S	L
A	O	E	I	T	U	K	T	R	F	R	P	M	D	E
K	P	O	O	G	C	E	K	E	E	Ö	A	E	A	F
E	N	E	P	U	A	R	R	F	E	S	L	S	L	F
E	T	A	Z	S	E	B	I	T	L	F	S	S	A	Ö
T	E	A	P	S	E	N	E	G	S	Ö	O	E	S	L
I	E	O	S	K	K	L	L	L	A	Z	F	R	M	E
L	O	A	H	K	I	A	B	I	L	Ö	L	F	K	E
N	W	Ü	A	G	S	N	O	A	T	O	P	A	E	T
K	L	E	S	S	Ü	H	C	S	T	A	L	A	S	L

____________	ESSLÖFFEL
______	GABEL
_______	GLAS
_______	LÖFFEL
______	MESSER
________ shaker	PFEFFERSTREUER
_______ bowl	SALATSCHÜSSEL
_____ shaker	SALZSTREUER
_______	SERVIETTE
_______ knife	STEAKMESSER
________	TEEKANNE
__________	TEELÖFFEL
______	TELLER
water ________	WASSERKRUG
_______ bowl	ZUCKERDOSE

REVIEW: TOOLS

104

Fill-in-the-Blanks: Find the missing translations hidden in the wordsearch grid and fill-in-the-blanks in the word list below. If you need some help, refer back to the original puzzle.

```
R E M M A H Z L O H A M M E R
U P D A S O T O S R T S Ä G E
T N L W M E E H H E E A A M H
Y B A I F U C C N D E H S R E
O R M G E N T A I D L C E N I
D A S O E R I T O A H V P S Z
I R L R S L S A E L I S Ä T N
D H W E R N I I Ü R T S E U E
N A E M I C Ü S D L N L I N B
A F R M O T S W O A L Y S N U
B N C A T E E B U A R H C S A
S O S H L R C R M A A G T F R
S N A T C Z G R L R N Ä W S H
E R U S A E M E P A T N I A C
M Z A N G E N E B U A R H C S
```

BOLTS
HAMMER
____
____
NAIL
____
PLIERS
____
____
____
TAPE MEASURE
____

____
____
LEITER
HOLZHAMMER
____
MUTTERN
____
SÄGE
SCHRAUBE
SCHRAUBENZIEHER
____
SCHLÜSSEL

REVIEW: CLOTHING

105

Mix & Match: The translations in the word list below have been scrambled. Draw lines between the left and right hand columns to line up the matching words.

G	S	D	A	S	H	A	N	D	S	C	H	U	H	E
U	B	T	N	T	N	E	C	K	T	I	E	T	O	S
Z	A	A	D	R	E	S	S	E	K	L	E	I	D	I
N	A	S	T	O	N	T	L	O	S	D	R	E	S	S
A	E	O	H	H	V	S	T	T	H	Ü	E	W	T	S
F	O	H	D	S	R	E	R	A	Ü	Y	E	H	A	T
A	P	T	E	S	H	O	S	E	W	S	T	G	E	R
L	U	M	K	H	H	O	B	T	T	A	G	N	I	U
H	E	C	U	S	U	A	E	E	N	M	R	I	A	M
C	O	T	N	R	J	H	N	S	J	A	C	K	E	P
S	T	F	R	A	T	E	C	D	R	J	P	C	I	F
B	Y	E	C	Ü	K	S	A	S	T	A	E	O	M	H
E	T	K	E	C	G	E	S	O	H	P	T	T	E	O
L	E	R	O	T	A	T	G	L	O	V	E	S	V	S
T	L	S	N	B	A	D	E	M	A	N	T	E	L	E

BATHROBE	BADEMANTEL
BELT	GÜRTEL
DRESS	HANDSCHUHE
GLOVES	HOSE
HAT	HUT
JACKET	JACKE
NECKTIE	KLEID
PAJAMAS	KRAWATTE
PANTS	SCHLAFANZUG
PANTY HOSE	SCHUHE
SHOES	SHORTS
SHORTS	SOCKEN
SOCKS	STRUMPF
STOCKING	STRUMPFHOSE
VEST	WESTE

REVIEW: CLOTHING 2

106

Fill-in-the-Blanks: Find the missing translations hidden in the wordsearch grid and fill-in-the-blanks in the word list below. If you need some help, refer back to the original puzzle.

L	S	R	E	D	N	E	P	S	U	S	K	C	O	R
E	R	O	G	K	J	E	A	N	S	A	H	U	S	E
T	K	R	E	T	L	R	D	A	A	N	O	T	K	G
N	S	T	I	E	F	E	L	P	S	D	S	S	I	Ä
A	N	T	L	T	R	T	I	A	I	A	H	H	R	R
M	L	G	F	W	A	R	N	D	R	L	T	I	T	T
N	R	T	E	A	I	D	N	A	U	E	S	R	I	N
E	B	A	D	E	A	N	Z	U	G	N	I	T	U	E
G	R	T	I	L	J	E	A	N	S	H	G	T	S	S
E	I	I	S	N	S	W	I	M	S	U	I	T	R	O
R	E	T	A	U	C	H	R	T	Z	F	O	R	S	H
W	F	C	L	N	T	O	E	N	W	O	T	I	T	H
S	S	B	E	O	A	E	A	M	B	O	O	H	O	O
S	H	B	L	O	U	S	E	T	D	E	B	S	A	S
E	H	C	S	Ä	W	R	E	T	N	U	H	T	L	E

BLOUSE ______
BOOTS ______
BOW TIE ______
BRIEFS ______
CLOTHING ______
JEANS ______
RAINCOAT ______
SANDALS ______
SHIRT ______
SKIRT ______
SUIT ______
SUSPENDERS ______
SWIM SUIT ______
T-SHIRT _-_____
UNDERWEAR ______

REVIEW: JEWELLERY

107

Fill-in-the-Blanks: Find the missing translations hidden in the wordsearch grid and fill-in-the-blanks in the word list below. If you need some help, refer back to the original puzzle.

L	S	T	I	W	M	O	P	A	L	H	O	D	Y	D
H	L	A	P	O	U	E	N	G	E	R	I	N	L	A
U	R	T	T	T	E	H	D	D	N	O	M	A	I	D
T	A	L	T	O	Ä	I	T	A	E	I	R	B	T	C
T	E	E	R	N	I	B	U	R	I	E	R	M	L	E
N	P	K	G	H	A	E	O	I	M	L	G	R	A	B
E	B	E	C	N	U	D	T	E	A	E	L	A	R	E
C	R	D	G	O	I	E	N	N	A	D	A	O	R	T
K	O	I	O	N	L	R	W	E	G	T	S	S	N	T
L	O	S	H	E	I	A	R	A	P	C	A	A	E	E
A	C	E	C	P	T	R	R	H	H	P	M	P	L	K
C	H	A	H	C	P	A	A	E	O	A	O	H	R	S
E	R	A	H	O	M	A	I	T	I	N	M	I	E	L
B	S	E	N	S	W	T	S	D	Y	B	U	R	P	A
T	O	P	A	Z	S	G	N	I	R	R	A	E	H	H

_______________ ANHÄNGER
_______________ ARMBAND
_______________ BROSCHE
_______________ DIAMANT
_______________ HALSKETTE
_______________ MEDAILLON
_______________ OHRRINGE
_______________ OPAL
_______________ PERLEN
_______________ RING
_______________ RUBIN
_______________ SAPHIR
_______________ SMARAGD
_______________ TOPAS
_______________ UHR

REVIEW: TOILETRIES

108

Fill-in-the-Blanks: Find the missing translations hidden in the wordsearch grid and fill-in-the-blanks in the word list below. If you need some help, refer back to the original puzzle.

B	R	U	S	H	A	M	P	O	O	E	T	S	A	P
O	B	B	E	T	S	R	Ü	B	N	H	A	Z	L	K
R	O	Z	A	R	I	A	T	A	A	P	A	I	C	O
E	L	E	N	S	E	S	W	A	N	H	O	I	H	N
S	B	I	T	E	S	C	R	H	N	M	T	A	C	T
P	A	E	P	O	T	S	L	S	T	S	E	O	M	A
I	T	L	L	P	P	T	E	I	P	U	N	L	U	K
N	S	F	S	Ü	E	I	N	I	P	D	O	Ü	N	T
K	A	H	L	P	D	N	L	A	I	P	M	M	D	L
L	P	U	A	E	E	B	S	T	R	M	E	R	W	I
E	N	F	A	M	M	N	I	T	A	O	Y	R	A	N
G	H	F	W	O	P	O	V	K	I	E	D	O	S	S
A	A	Ö	C	N	N	O	A	C	R	F	I	O	S	E
N	Z	N	D	E	O	D	O	R	A	N	T	L	E	N
L	T	A	R	A	P	P	A	R	E	I	S	A	R	D

COMB	______
CONDITIONER	______________
contact LENSES	______________
dental ______	ZAHNSEIDE
______________	DEODORANT
hair ______	FÖN
______________	LIPPENSTIFT
MOUTHWASH	______________
nail ______	NAGELKNIPSER
RAZOR	______________
SHAMPOO	______________
tooth ______	ZAHNBÜRSTE
toothPASTE	______________

REVIEW: SPORTS

109

Mix & Match: The translations in the word list below have been scrambled. Draw lines between the left and right hand columns to line up the matching words.

I	F	N	G	Y	W	S	B	A	S	E	B	A	L	L
L	L	A	B	Y	E	L	L	O	V	I	F	T	E	G
I	H	B	W	O	M	N	S	O	U	U	N	I	D	N
S	W	I	M	M	I	N	G	U	A	H	P	N	R	I
V	O	L	L	E	Y	B	A	L	L	S	P	I	E	L
S	H	T	Y	B	O	B	T	S	L	A	N	S	G	T
C	O	L	R	X	A	S	O	L	T	G	H	N	L	S
H	E	C	I	O	N	S	A	X	E	I	I	F	L	E
W	Ä	N	C	U	P	B	K	N	E	C	C	R	A	R
I	G	P	K	E	T	S	T	E	N	N	I	S	B	W
M	O	S	G	E	R	Ä	T	E	T	U	R	N	E	N
M	I	W	K	T	D	E	F	H	C	B	H	R	S	E
E	I	S	K	A	T	I	N	G	C	I	A	F	A	E
N	A	Ä	E	I	S	H	O	C	K	E	Y	L	B	A
B	G	R	V	T	L	L	A	B	ß	U	F	L	L	A

BASEBALL	BASEBALL
BASKETBALL	BASKETBALLSPIEL
BOXING	BOXEN
FENCING	EISHOCKEY
figure SKATING	EISKUNSTLAUF
GYMNASTICS	FECHTSPORT
ICE hockey	FUßBALL
SOCCER	GERÄTETURNEN
SWIMMING	RINGEN
TENNIS	SCHWIMMEN
VOLLEYBALL	TENNIS
WRESTLING	VOLLEYBALLSPIEL

REVIEW: SPORTS 2

110

Fill-in-the-Blanks: Find the missing translations hidden in the wordsearch grid and fill-in-the-blanks in the word list below. If you need some help, refer back to the original puzzle.

E	I	S	S	C	H	N	E	L	L	L	A	U	F	W
G	N	U	R	P	S	T	I	E	W	G	M	U	G	A
N	G	S	I	V	A	D	I	L	N	H	A	C	N	S
U	N	I	V	C	A	L	I	I	E	L	H	E	U	S
R	U	N	S	T	U	U	I	V	G	V	T	E	R	E
P	R	N	E	G	E	K	L	N	I	T	A	T	P	R
S	P	E	E	D	S	K	A	T	I	N	G	J	S	B
H	S	T	N	T	D	L	C	L	R	H	G	I	H	A
C	I	H	F	N	I	A	H	I	I	I	N	I	C	L
O	E	C	H	K	R	C	S	O	R	N	P	D	O	L
H	R	S	S	A	S	O	E	I	E	C	I	L	H	S
B	D	I	P	B	P	L	D	T	A	S	D	A	E	P
A	R	T	O	E	O	O	T	E	K	C	I	R	C	I
T	C	B	I	N	E	P	D	E	L	S	B	O	B	E
S	N	E	G	N	I	R	P	S	T	S	N	U	K	L

BOBSLED ______________
CRICKET ________
cross country SKIING ____________
DIVING ______________
HIGH jump ____________
JAVELIN ______
LONG jump ___________
LUGE ___________
pole VAULT ________________
SPEED SKATING ______________
table TENNIS ____________
TRIPLE jump ____________
water POLO ________________

REVIEW: PLACES

111

Fill-in-the-Blanks: Find the missing translations hidden in the wordsearch grid and fill-in-the-blanks in the word list below. If you need some help, refer back to the original puzzle.

T	E	E	E	S	U	P	E	R	M	A	R	K	E	T
N	K	S	O	O	R	A	I	R	P	O	R	T	F	B
E	C	B	T	M	A	T	S	O	P	A	M	W	O	A
M	Ü	E	Ü	A	B	M	S	T	N	O	U	N	H	R
T	R	F	M	R	D	T	U	K	D	T	E	O	D	E
R	B	U	I	E	O	I	E	S	S	W	S	I	E	T
A	E	D	T	F	T	N	U	U	E	P	U	D	I	A
P	G	C	F	T	H	A	P	M	I	U	M	A	R	E
E	H	I	I	A	H	E	R	T	T	N	M	T	F	H
D	C	I	U	F	R	C	A	Y	R	A	M	S	P	T
E	X	S	U	M	F	L	U	G	H	A	F	E	N	E
C	I	A	A	D	H	O	A	E	L	U	H	C	S	I
A	K	R	S	C	H	O	O	L	L	L	C	O	O	V
I	K	I	N	O	C	A	T	H	E	D	R	A	L	O
T	E	H	E	L	I	G	H	T	H	O	U	S	E	M

____	BAR
______	BRÜCKE
______	BÜRO
__________	DOM
_______	FLUGHAFEN
_________	FRIEDHOF
___________ store	KAUFHAUS
_____ ______	KINO
________	KRANKENHAUS
__________	LEUCHTTURM
______	MUSEUM
____ _____	POSTAMT
______	SCHULE
______	STADION
___________	SUPERMARKT

REVIEW: PLACES 2

112

Fill-in-the-Blanks: Find the missing translations hidden in the wordsearch grid and fill-in-the-blanks in the word list below. If you need some help, refer back to the original puzzle.

```
W R L C U N I V E R S I T Ä T
P E T I C Z T A L P K R A P F
A S H T B H A B N E F A H W Ä
R T I Y A R A T H A U S R L H
K A D H N N A T O I S U E O C
T U O A K E O R R S N T T H S
O R G L T I L O Y I O E A O E
L A T L L S B T V H L K E P G
G N S B T R N E S S L E H E R
N T I O A O R E T A E H T R U
I B R H T S O E N E C T R N B
K E A S I N W O T N W O D H T
R E S T A U R A N T I P A A S
A T Y C A M R A H P G A I U W
P A R K N O P E R A H O U S E
```

BANK	______
CASTLE	______
CITY HALL	______
______	INNENSTADT
______	HAFEN
HOTEL	______
______	BIBLIOTHEK
OPERA HOUSE	______
PARK	______
PARKING LOT	______
______	APOTHEKE
______	RESTAURANT
STORE	______
THEATER	______
UNIVERSITY	______

REVIEW: PLACES 3

113

Mix & Match: The translations in the word list below have been scrambled. Draw lines between the left and right hand columns to line up the matching words.

N	T	S	T	E	M	M	O	S	C	H	E	E	É	G
E	F	H	B	H	H	A	F	É	U	G	N	D	F	L
M	O	S	Q	U	E	C	D	L	O	B	A	H	A	A
B	H	B	S	T	S	D	R	G	O	M	W	C	C	I
U	N	F	A	B	A	B	A	I	M	R	H	A	Z	F
C	H	E	E	O	L	N	A	O	K	U	I	T	Y	I
H	A	U	E	R	Y	U	E	H	R	K	A	S	E	R
H	B	E	B	S	O	E	M	C	N	L	H	C	T	E
A	O	R	Y	A	F	T	H	E	P	H	I	B	U	S
N	W	W	G	F	H	S	S	F	N	L	O	A	S	T
D	L	A	O	N	T	N	L	K	O	L	O	F	R	A
L	I	C	O	F	L	O	G	P	O	I	A	P	Y	T
U	N	H	A	B	G	N	I	L	W	O	B	D	Y	I
N	G	E	U	G	O	G	A	N	Y	S	B	I	E	O
G	R	E	I	V	E	R	I	E	Z	I	L	O	P	N

BOOKSTORE	BAHNHOF
BOWLING alley	BLUMENLADEN
BUS station	BOWLINGBAHN
CHURCH	BUCHHANDLUNG
COFFEE shop	BUSBAHNHOF
DAM	CAFÉ
FIRE STATION	DAMM
FLORIST	FEUERWACHE
GOLF course	GOLFPLATZ
MOSQUE	KIRCHE
POLICE station	MOSCHEE
RAILROAD station	POLIZEIREVIER
SUBWAY station	SYNAGOGE
SYNAGOGUE	U-BAHN-station

REVIEW: ON THE ROAD

114

Fill-in-the-Blanks: Find the missing translations hidden in the wordsearch grid and fill-in-the-blanks in the word list below. If you need some help, refer back to the original puzzle.

N H A B N E ß A R T S E S S Z

M R W C T M C P I C K U P R D

O I R H O Y A F O M B R V D S

T N F P C S T A T I O N E U N

O L E ß N O C I N R E R B V E

R D M G S H N I T G A E K L G

R S O M A I M V A S S C I W A

A R T B I W O W E I U B B A W

D E O R U N T T E R O O M G E

Ä O R M O S I R T M T H O E D

I I C H A P T V O U H I K N N

E W Y L B U S T A P H T B R Ä

P I C K U P U A H N S S T L L

O B L O R A C T E E R T S W E

T T E L O I R B A K A G Y E G

AUTOMOBILE ______

BUS ____

CAR _______

COACH _________

CONVERTIBLE ___________

MINIVAN _______

MOPED ____

MOTORCYCLE __________

PICKUP truck _______

SPORTS car ____________

SUV ______________

STATION wagon ______

STREETCAR ____________

TRUCK ___________

REVIEW: VEHICLES

115

Fill-in-the-Blanks: Find the missing translations hidden in the wordsearch grid and fill-in-the-blanks in the word list below. If you need some help, refer back to the original puzzle.

P	B	N	F	H	M	S	U	B	Y	W	H	O	Y	P
L	O	O	E	R	E	C	N	A	L	U	B	M	A	A
O	T	L	O	G	S	L	W	R	B	N	D	N	L	N
O	O	L	I	T	A	B	I	S	N	D	H	Ö	I	Z
H	O	I	E	Z	U	W	C	C	A	I	S	A	S	E
C	B	N	P	S	E	H	S	R	O	C	A	C	B	R
S	E	I	N	O	R	I	R	G	H	P	H	R	K	U
U	E	E	C	A	L	H	F	F	N	U	T	C	T	C
B	S	N	U	Y	A	I	A	A	L	U	U	E	A	T
M	R	B	G	F	C	H	C	B	H	R	T	N	R	A
A	E	U	U	P	R	L	U	E	T	R	O	T	M	O
R	T	S	Z	Z	K	S	E	E	C	E	Z	F	E	B
I	N	P	E	N	A	I	R	P	L	A	N	E	U	R
N	U	U	A	E	E	I	K	A	N	U	R	L	U	O
E	G	T	T	H	F	I	F	L	U	G	Z	E	U	G

______	BOOT
________	FAHRRAD
________	FLUGZEUG
__________	HUBSCHRAUBER
______	KANU
city ____	LINIENBUS
____ ______	LÖSCHFAHRZEUG
______	PANZER
______ ____	POLIZEIFAHRZEUG
__________	RETTUNGSWAGEN
________ bus	SCHULBUS
________	U-BAHN
__________	UNTERSEEBOOT
______	ZUG

REVIEW: LANGUAGES

116

Fill-in-the-Blanks: Find the missing translations hidden in the wordsearch grid and fill-in-the-blanks in the word list below. If you need some help, refer back to the original puzzle.

```
H G A T P O L N I S C H C H K
W C N H E N I M S N P C C R E
C T S A C R R P A O S S E S E
C I C I A S A U R N I I E O R
A N B D S N I T S S D N E A G
T R N A I Ö U N E S A A U G S
H A A S R G Z I E P I P R R P
M C C B U A G N A I L A T I A
N H S E I U C J A D L J N E N
Y A S I T S P G E R M A N C I
T E E R S O C U T Y F I T H S
H E O R L S T H C N E R F I H
A P I I O S U S E N G L I S H
I N S Ö C K O R E A N I S C H
C H S H O A E N G L I S C H E
```

______
ENGLISH
FRENCH
______
______
______
______
______
______
POLISH
______
______
SPANISH
THAI

ARABISCH
______
______
DEUTSCH
GRIECHISCH
ITALIENISCH
JAPANISCH
KOREANISCH
MANDARIN
______
PORTUGIESISCH
RUSSISCH
______
______

REVIEW: LANGUAGES 2

117

Mix & Match: The translations in the word list below have been scrambled. Draw lines between the left and right hand columns to line up the matching words.

E	T	N	N	A	I	S	R	E	P	A	S	D	R	H
B	V	U	H	C	S	I	D	E	W	H	C	S	H	H
U	E	I	R	D	O	I	R	H	C	K	H	I	C	C
L	R	O	E	K	R	S	L	S	I	I	S	S	H	S
G	E	F	L	T	I	U	I	I	D	N	I	H	E	I
A	I	S	I	S	N	S	M	S	H	D	D	S	B	K
R	H	N	C	N	E	A	H	Ä	N	A	E	I	R	R
I	S	H	D	N	N	E	M	Ä	N	M	W	A	Ä	Ü
S	I	U	O	O	B	I	L	E	A	I	S	S	I	T
C	N	D	A	R	N	R	S	N	S	E	S	R	S	T
H	N	I	E	H	E	E	T	C	R	I	T	C	C	S
I	I	W	C	D	E	E	S	R	H	O	S	L	H	U
Ü	F	T	E	N	I	L	H	I	I	M	O	C	D	E
I	U	I	W	V	N	A	I	N	A	M	O	R	H	S
D	N	A	I	R	A	G	L	U	B	N	U	R	D	U

BULGARIAN	BULGARISCH
DUTCH	FINNISCH
FINNISH	HEBRÄISCH
HEBREW	HINDI
HINDI	INDONESISCH
INDONESIAN	NIEDERLÄNDISCH
PERSIAN	PERSISCH
ROMANIAN	RUMÄNISCH
SWAHILI	SCHWEDISCH
SWEDISH	SUAHELI
TURKISH	TÜRKISCH
URDU	URDU
VIETNAMESE	VIETNAMESISCH

REVIEW: PROFESSIONS

118

Fill-in-the-Blanks: Find the missing translations hidden in the wordsearch grid and fill-in-the-blanks in the word list below. If you need some help, refer back to the original puzzle.

T	E	Ü	R	E	Y	W	A	L	P	G	T	H	Y	N
Z	K	E	P	T	N	I	U	S	N	N	C	R	R	P
R	L	Ü	R	S	C	G	Y	F	N	D	E	E	O	R
A	E	L	C	H	Y	C	I	A	E	L	T	L	T	E
N	H	C	E	H	H	C	M	N	E	K	I	E	C	K
H	R	F	H	I	E	R	H	I	E	Z	H	C	O	I
A	E	E	A	T	E	N	P	I	E	E	C	T	D	R
Z	R	T	T	M	S	S	C	I	A	T	R	R	E	T
T	E	O	M	N	U	A	B	H	L	T	A	I	N	K
R	L	I	T	A	E	E	N	P	E	O	R	C	T	E
A	Z	S	H	C	A	P	H	W	O	F	T	I	I	L
T	E	C	R	M	A	R	R	P	A	L	Ü	A	S	E
T	S	N	T	O	L	I	P	A	O	L	I	N	T	T
R	U	E	I	N	E	G	N	I	C	N	T	C	A	S
A	R	C	H	I	T	E	K	T	E	A	C	H	E	R

ACTOR ____________
ARCHITECT ____________
CARPENTER ____________
CHEF ____________
DENTIST ____________
DOCTOR ______
ELECTRICIAN ____________
ENGINEER ____________
LAWYER ____________
PILOT ______
POLICE officer ____________
PSYCHIATRIST ____________
TEACHER ________

REVIEW: SOLAR SYSTEM

119

Fill-in-the-Blanks: Find the missing translations hidden in the wordsearch grid and fill-in-the-blanks in the word list below. If you need some help, refer back to the original puzzle.

S	I	N	R	E	T	S	N	I	F	T	D	M	E	H
H	L	O	R	E	T	I	P	U	J	R	A	A	D	M
Y	R	P	O	C	R	R	L	R	S	R	V	E	E	E
I	R	M	N	T	M	L	R	A	S	E	O	D	R	T
S	P	U	O	E	M	A	E	N	N	O	S	L	F	S
O	R	A	C	O	O	T	R	U	K	R	E	M	E	Y
L	E	D	O	R	N	T	S	S	E	M	O	N	D	S
A	B	N	C	N	E	U	T	D	S	C	T	C	S	N
R	H	O	U	U	O	M	R	A	R	N	U	P	E	E
S	C	M	O	T	R	E	T	A	R	K	L	T	A	N
Y	A	L	U	P	P	U	T	U	N	H	P	P	R	N
S	T	L	E	E	R	E	T	I	P	U	J	A	T	O
T	P	O	D	N	R	A	N	E	C	H	S	L	H	S
E	S	V	I	R	S	U	N	E	V	L	A	S	E	E
M	O	S	T	O	T	A	L	E	C	L	I	P	S	E

______ ERDE
______ JUPITER
______ KRATER
______ MARS
______ MERKUR
______ MOND
______ NEPTUN
______ PLUTO
______ SATURN
______ SONNE
______ ______ SONNENSYSTEM
______ ______ totale FINSTERNIS
______ URANUS
______ VENUS
______ ______ VOLLMOND

REVIEW: INSTRUMENTS

120

Fill-in-the-Blanks: Find the missing translations hidden in the wordsearch grid and fill-in-the-blanks in the word list below. If you need some help, refer back to the original puzzle.

```
A B U T L N D R U M S O E W E
B N O E D R O K K A S H E N A
U L A P B L O I X T O A A S K
T E O M O R I O D S G E S E I
T M T U N N P D L R N N O P N
A M D R G H A A N N O D H I O
M O U T O E B I L H B C S P M
B R D N S M R E P E E A C G R
O T E P Y U P O N L G O O A A
U W L C B P X E L I D Ü T B H
R R S M E A K O T C L I L P D
I E A R S C F A F E U O U F N
N T C I E I R O R G E L I U U
E A K B O R G A N I L O I V M
D O L L E C H A R M O N I C A
```

____
BAGPIPES
BONGOS
CELLO
____
DRUMS
GUITAR
HARMONICA
____
____
____
____
____
TUBA
____

AKKORDEON
____
____
____
BECKEN
____
____
____
ORGEL
FLÜGEL
SAXOPHON
TAMBURIN
TROMPETE
____
VIOLINE

RANDOM REVIEW

121

Random Review: The word list below has been randomly selected from the words covered in this book. Draw lines between the right and left columns to match the words with their translations. Good luck!

N	H	E	T	F	R	A	N	Z	Ö	S	I	S	C	H
T	E	A	R	R	G	O	A	T	T	D	O	I	C	I
B	R	A	C	E	L	E	T	D	E	L	P	H	I	N
O	W	R	R	N	K	E	F	L	Ö	A	I	U	Z	T
U	U	C	S	C	A	C	S	L	F	S	O	I	H	T
N	N	H	T	H	H	B	U	O	Ü	D	E	C	T	O
I	B	I	N	E	O	I	M	Z	K	G	S	I	T	E
V	L	T	V	B	W	P	T	D	E	I	E	S	N	F
E	E	E	A	E	E	O	E	E	S	H	R	L	D	E
R	G	C	P	L	R	P	L	R	K	I	S	P	N	E
S	B	T	R	N	O	S	E	L	S	T	U	T	A	T
I	E	E	I	M	T	P	I	L	E	I	G	Ü	B	C
T	S	B	C	P	O	U	L	T	R	Y	A	A	M	Ö
Ä	T	D	O	L	P	H	I	N	Y	A	R	N	R	U
T	N	E	T	T	I	L	H	C	S	B	O	B	A	R

APRICOT
ARCHITECT
BOBSLED
BRACELET
DOLPHIN
FRENCH
GOAT
MOPED
PERSIAN
POULTRY
SUGAR
TEA
TO BE
UNIVERSITY
YELLOW

APRIKOSE
ARCHITEKT
ARMBAND
BOBSCHLITTEN
DELPHIN
FRANZÖSISCH
GEFLÜGEL
GELB
MOFA
PERSISCH
SEIN
TEE
UNIVERSITÄT
ZIEGE
ZUCKER

RANDOM REVIEW

122

Random Review: The word list below has been randomly selected from the words covered in this book. Find the missing translations hidden in the wordsearch grid and fill-in-the-blanks in the word list below. Good luck!

E	G	E	F	R	I	E	R	E	N	D	E	R	M	M
D	L	H	R	L	M	T	R	E	T	T	E	V	U	G
N	G	E	E	N	I	U	I	E	S	A	N	S	E	T
E	T	N	E	I	I	N	S	C	F	I	C	M	N	M
N	S	O	Z	S	L	O	K	K	G	L	C	N	I	E
E	M	O	I	U	H	B	S	N	E	G	O	E	E	S
H	C	S	N	O	P	A	U	S	A	L	W	W	B	U
C	I	E	G	C	T	H	L	T	F	B	N	D	N	A
O	G	P	W	U	T	E	S	I	T	E	N	R	R	M
W	M	I	R	N	G	M	E	A	B	E	E	L	H	R
N	R	D	A	R	A	T	B	B	K	U	E	E	Y	E
O	A	T	A	S	U	H	U	E	A	U	T	G	N	D
Y	E	P	R	U	G	H	E	O	F	N	H	M	T	E
E	S	A	O	E	E	W	O	L	F	O	K	I	A	L
A	S	P	A	R	A	G	U	S	T	E	C	N	N	F

ASPARAGUS ________
BANK _____
BAT ___________
COUSIN _______
COW ___
EYE _____
FREEZING rain _____________ regen
HALIBUT ________
LEG ____
MUSCLES ________
NOSE _____
ONE ___
SATURDAY ________
WEEKEND ___________
WOLF _____

RANDOM REVIEW

1 2 3

Random Review: The word list below has been randomly selected from the words covered in this book. Find the missing translations hidden in the wordsearch grid and fill-in-the-blanks in the word list below. Good luck!

F	I	S	H	R	E	N	N	E	N	I	V	T	Z	A
A	G	Ü	R	T	E	L	H	C	B	E	E	R	N	L
C	S	D	H	N	B	C	P	H	C	E	A	B	S	E
I	S	A	M	R	S	L	Ü	I	F	W	L	A	H	T
R	E	M	M	I	Z	F	A	L	H	C	S	T	O	N
E	N	E	F	H	T	O	A	C	I	E	I	H	E	A
M	O	R	O	E	D	M	S	D	K	B	Y	R	S	M
A	S	I	I	G	I	R	R	R	E	N	E	O	L	E
H	D	K	S	N	N	A	A	D	T	E	K	B	E	D
T	N	A	G	C	V	I	R	V	B	T	N	E	K	A
U	A	O	U	E	H	O	M	M	E	I	O	D	N	B
O	R	I	L	E	O	U	O	A	A	L	D	R	E	N
S	G	U	S	M	Ü	R	H	R	L	U	U	E	U	T
N	O	E	K	S	B	S	B	E	A	F	E	O	E	N
B	L	A	C	K	B	E	R	R	I	E	S	H	B	A

______ BADEMANTEL
______ BOULEVARD
______ BROMBEEREN
______ ENKEL
______ ESEL
______ FISCHE
______ FLAMINGO
______ GEHIRN
______ GÜRTEL
______ HÜFTE
______ ______ RENNEN
______ SCHLAFZIMMER
______ SCHUHE
______ SCHWARZ
______ ______ SÜDAMERIKA

RANDOM REVIEW

124

Random Review: The word list below has been randomly selected from the words covered in this book. Find the missing translations hidden in the wordsearch grid and fill-in-the-blanks in the word list below. Good luck!

R	M	D	A	T	E	H	U	H	C	S	D	N	A	H
E	S	U	O	L	B	I	N	G	U	A	H	M	O	Y
D	A	I	S	A	G	S	A	T	F	Y	U	T	H	A
L	P	L	S	E	P	T	E	M	B	E	R	Y	L	D
U	B	M	O	K	U	X	I	P	S	Y	L	G	S	E
O	D	L	N	C	A	M	R	U	T	U	A	S	B	G
H	N	N	U	A	U	E	M	T	O	E	K	L	E	I
S	O	C	A	S	T	B	I	R	C	C	M	A	C	T
H	G	I	O	L	E	U	A	S	E	E	S	B	K	T
O	A	R	U	E	S	N	G	T	E	I	P	M	E	E
L	T	H	I	D	G	I	H	N	E	V	O	Y	N	R
E	C	E	E	U	E	C	A	N	A	U	O	C	O	B
S	O	O	T	D	A	L	G	E	N	R	L	L	D	E
N	N	A	S	E	P	I	P	G	A	B	O	H	G	T
I	N	E	K	C	E	B	M	M	I	W	H	C	S	T

______
ASIA
BAGPIPES
______
CRIB
______
DAY
GLOVES
ISLAND
MUSEUM
______
ORANGUTAN
______
SEPTEMBER
SHOULDER

ALGEN
______
______
BLUSE
______
BECKEN
______
______
______
______
ACHTECK
______ - ______
SCHWIMMBECKEN
______
______

RANDOM REVIEW

Random Review: The word list below has been randomly selected from the words covered in this book. Draw lines between the right and left columns to match the words with their translations. Good luck!

W	N	H	A	H	R	E	S	S	A	W	V	T	S	N
N	N	Ö	Y	N	E	T	A	M	I	R	P	K	H	E
H	C	U	M	A	O	L	R	D	R	D	N	A	H	H
U	H	S	T	Z	W	A	I	U	D	S	B	L	A	C
B	I	E	Y	P	U	B	A	C	Y	U	N	A	N	N
S	P	T	T	N	E	M	U	N	O	M	E	M	D	R
C	M	A	T	R	A	N	A	S	E	P	P	K	H	Ö
H	U	M	M	I	N	G	B	I	R	D	T	N	T	H
R	N	I	L	W	O	L	O	T	A	E	U	E	A	N
A	K	R	Y	G	S	N	E	G	S	A	N	D	R	E
U	R	P	U	E	E	J	B	M	E	E	E	E	S	K
B	T	E	C	U	A	F	U	R	M	A	U	T	O	C
E	I	T	E	H	I	R	B	I	L	O	K	N	A	A
R	E	G	R	M	D	S	B	I	O	I	R	A	U	B
U	E	L	I	B	O	M	O	T	U	A	N	T	A	E

AUNT	AUTO
AUTOMOBILE	BACKENHÖRNCHEN
CHIPMUNK	DENKMAL
DRUMS	HAND
FAUCET	HUBSCHRAUBER
HAND	JAHR
HELICOPTER	KOLIBRI
HUMMINGBIRD	MEER
MONUMENT	NEPTUN
NEPTUNE	PRIMATEN
PRIMATES	SYNAGOGE
SEA	TANTE
SUBWAY	TROMMELN
SYNAGOGUE	U-BAHN
YEAR	WASSERHAHN

RANDOM REVIEW

126

Random Review: The word list below has been randomly selected from the words covered in this book. Find the missing translations hidden in the wordsearch grid and fill-in-the-blanks in the word list below. Good luck!

A	S	D	Y	B	I	B	L	I	O	T	H	E	K	R
L	T	W	E	N	T	Y	D	A	I	H	L	C	H	S
C	N	H	E	Z	L	O	I	Ä	L	O	U	N	A	A
R	M	Z	U	I	S	N	R	I	B	D	E	L	D	I
Ä	E	W	M	M	O	D	B	S	D	G	I	C	W	I
K	R	A	K	E	M	R	T	R	N	H	I	E	I	T
N	F	N	F	K	A	E	A	I	E	F	K	G	Ä	A
R	A	Z	U	R	R	N	R	B	B	D	F	A	L	L
W	E	I	Y	L	B	O	R	Ä	I	N	U	T	S	I
E	I	G	L	O	E	Ä	W	T	H	E	L	N	E	E
R	L	E	M	A	I	D	N	O	M	L	L	O	V	N
B	I	S	E	S	T	U	N	D	T	D	M	M	S	I
E	M	R	C	T	E	I	I	O	C	T	O	P	U	S
H	A	H	M	O	N	D	A	Y	T	R	O	A	D	C
N	F	C	B	W	R	E	S	T	L	I	N	G	E	H

DUCK ______
FAMILY ________
FULL MOON ____________
HEBREW ____________
ITALIAN ____________
LIBRARY ____________
LOBSTER _________
MONDAY _________
OCTOPUS ________
RED _____
TEN ______
TO DO ____
TO WORK __________
TWENTY _________
WRESTLING ________

RANDOM REVIEW

127

Random Review: The word list below has been randomly selected from the words covered in this book. Find the missing translations hidden in the wordsearch grid and fill-in-the-blanks in the word list below. Good luck!

I	E	H	C	Ä	L	F	D	N	A	H	E	A	D	S
G	S	C	Y	O	N	E	H	E	S	S	E	A	E	C
E	B	U	I	Y	F	Ä	E	I	E	E	T	K	K	H
Ü	T	A	M	U	N	F	E	V	P	O	H	O	U	R
Ä	B	H	B	M	J	B	E	E	S	A	P	M	S	A
L	E	M	L	O	E	N	Y	E	B	F	V	B	T	U
E	T	A	H	N	O	R	E	M	M	O	S	I	E	B
N	P	I	G	U	A	N	A	A	S	A	L	D	A	E
A	O	E	V	M	R	A	D	N	N	Ü	D	T	A	N
C	R	I	E	É	T	R	O	A	D	S	N	T	S	E
I	E	S	T	F	S	S	I	R	E	O	A	E	A	Ä
R	O	S	M	A	R	I	N	K	Ü	H	U	M	N	N
R	H	T	F	C	T	A	Ü	F	A	N	G	S	A	T
U	I	T	R	E	I	S	L	S	C	N	E	W	Y	S
H	E	N	I	T	S	E	T	N	I	L	L	A	M	S

________ shop	CAFÉ
______ _________	DÜNNDARM
_____	HANDFLÄCHE
__________	HURRIKAN
________ wagon	KOMBI
_____	KOPF
______	LEGUAN
_______	PAVIAN
___________	ROSMARIN
_____	SAFT
______	SCHRAUBEN
__ ___	SEHEN
______	SIEBEN
____	SOHN
_______	SOMMER

RANDOM REVIEW

128

Random Review: The word list below has been randomly selected from the words covered in this book. Find the missing translations hidden in the wordsearch grid and fill-in-the-blanks in the word list below. Good luck!

H	T	N	E	N	E	V	N	J	R	N	E	S	S	D
E	T	H	R	E	E	O	E	C	A	R	L	R	D	R
R	Y	A	L	P	O	T	C	I	A	G	M	Ö	V	E
B	T	B	E	H	O	S	R	U	G	R	U	E	C	I
S	A	E	P	S	T	E	G	I	A	H	I	A	R	S
T	T	Y	E	O	N	A	V	A	E	N	T	B	R	P
R	T	W	S	T	J	O	U	A	S	R	E	E	O	R
I	T	I	I	W	H	T	B	N	E	S	D	I	E	U
P	P	E	N	O	U	F	S	E	E	L	Ö	W	E	N
L	R	Y	A	M	A	H	W	A	G	L	O	R	H	G
E	O	R	N	H	Ö	H	L	G	E	E	E	T	D	G
J	V	P	R	O	V	I	N	C	E	Y	S	I	A	R
U	I	E	H	S	O	H	C	S	I	T	R	I	P	N
M	N	Ö	A	N	U	F	I	A	T	J	L	U	N	S
P	Z	Ä	H	N	E	Y	N	H	E	Z	T	H	C	A

ANISE
AUTUMN
______
EIGHTEEN
JAGUAR
PROVINCE
SEA LION
TABLE
TEETH
THREE
___ ______
TRIPLE JUMP
____
VEINS

______
RENTIER
____
____
____
____
______
______
ABFAHREN
SPIELEN
____
TAIFUN
______

RANDOM REVIEW

129

Random Review: The word list below has been randomly selected from the words covered in this book. Draw lines between the right and left columns to match the words with their translations. Good luck!

W	N	S	A	P	E	C	W	I	N	D	O	W	P	A
C	O	N	E	G	N	A	Z	O	U	F	D	S	V	N
I	E	O	R	S	C	S	E	P	E	A	N	E	U	A
L	L	S	D	I	Q	L	H	N	M	E	N	O	T	E
R	E	O	R	P	Ä	U	S	E	H	U	M	P	H	N
A	M	F	N	M	E	T	I	C	E	S	I	E	C	A
G	A	A	A	J	E	C	N	R	R	P	T	L	E	R
I	H	H	A	R	N	R	K	E	R	Y	T	I	P	R
N	C	H	Ö	S	Ö	U	I	E	H	E	E	K	S	E
A	R	S	C	H	U	L	T	E	R	B	L	A	T	T
C	E	P	H	L	P	A	L	L	E	E	M	N	R	I
I	H	C	U	A	L	B	O	N	K	E	E	H	T	D
L	I	L	F	A	L	E	T	T	U	C	E	E	T	E
E	Ä	O	S	C	H	A	F	A	K	I	R	F	A	M
P	S	H	O	U	L	D	E	R	B	L	A	D	E	U

AFRICA	AFRIKA
AVENUE	ALLEE
CHAMELEON	CHAMÄLEON
GARLIC	EICHHÖRNCHEN
LETTUCE	FENSTER
MEDITERRANEAN sea	JAHR
PELICAN	KNOBLAUCH
PLIERS	MITTELMEER
SHEEP	PELIKAN
SHOULDER BLADE	SALAT
SOFA	SCHAF
SQUIRREL	SCHULTERBLATT
WINDOW	SOFA
WOODPECKER	SPECHT
YEAR	ZANGEN

RANDOM REVIEW

130

Random Review: The word list below has been randomly selected from the words covered in this book. Find the missing translations hidden in the wordsearch grid and fill-in-the-blanks in the word list below. Good luck!

N	A	Y	C	D	H	C	S	I	R	A	G	L	U	B
A	B	E	N	D	E	N	O	K	L	A	B	S	L	T
C	U	T	W	O	G	R	R	U	R	N	T	P	C	O
R	L	R	E	A	G	O	D	Ä	G	R	ß	R	H	R
Y	G	E	N	M	S	F	F	N	A	A	E	N	T	E
N	A	D	K	T	P	S	A	ß	U	A	R	A	B	P
P	R	N	G	N	T	L	E	O	M	H	N	Y	A	P
U	I	U	E	R	E	E	E	R	E	O	E	Z	L	E
M	A	H	E	M	V	H	S	N	M	B	B	N	C	P
A	N	E	O	E	U	O	C	X	H	E	R	A	O	W
T	T	C	N	N	T	A	H	S	H	A	L	O	N	O
H	H	I	E	S	M	U	L	P	R	R	S	O	Y	L
I	N	H	T	N	O	M	Ä	F	E	E	T	E	N	L
G	E	L	B	E	R	H	F	I	P	I	B	R	A	E
H	N	O	L	E	M	R	E	T	A	W	U	O	R	Y

BALCONY ________
BULGARIAN ____________
COUGAR ______
CREAM _______
CYAN ______
EGGS _____
EVENING _______
MONTH _______
ONE HUNDRED _________
PLUMS __________
STREET ________
TEMPLE _________
THIGH ________________
YELLOW PEPPER ________ paprika
WATERMELON ________________

RANDOM REVIEW

131

Random Review: The word list below has been randomly selected from the words covered in this book. Find the missing translations hidden in the wordsearch grid and fill-in-the-blanks in the word list below. Good luck!

```
R E T M ß I A P B E L C T T S
E A P A H W T O I E I O G A R
D R C S T O H H L N U O L V E
A R U T E N S E O N S T E P D
R I E D E E V E D U P R O D N
R N K A K E D E N A S L A H E
O G N R N Ü R N S T N A A P P
T S A M T S C T E I R B N P S
O A E N T E I H S S N Ä O D U
M L B A S N E C E E U L G L S
U Z N L A N H E ß N I A T E Ü
T D E K S T U A H S C N T D R
C U E G N I R R H O E H I E R
E T R M O T O R C Y C L E K D
R E G E S O O G T C H E F F S
```

________	ELF
________	GANS
______ ____	grüne BOHNE
_____	HAUT
_____________	HOSENTRÄGER
______	KÜCHENCHEF
________	MASTDARM
_____________	MOTORRAD
__________	OHRRINGE
________	PASTINAKE
_______	POLNISCH
_____	SALZ
________	STRAßENBAHN
________	TAUSEND
__ ________	VERSTEHEN

RANDOM REVIEW

132

Random Review: The word list below has been randomly selected from the words covered in this book. Find the missing translations hidden in the wordsearch grid and fill-in-the-blanks in the word list below. Good luck!

```
V S E M D R E D N A M A L A S
B T O W A L K T I N R G ß E T
T A E I T R I N K E N U F A E
G I D M S U I U T H S B W N R
ß R U E S I Y E U E Ü Y E I M
V S S M A T T I N G O D A S I
G I I H R N L Ü N K A A A N T
E W E O T E Z I M L Ä L H S E
S R F R H O R U N M A F I D R
C T E C Z P D E G M L R E S M
H R N L S I M R A D O E A R I
Ä E N H L U G N I L H Ü R F T
F P E A L E D C F N P L A T E
T P L B N E T I H W K A H L M
N E P O R P O I S E R O T S D
```

____
____
____
LADYBUG
____
____
SALAMANDER
____
____
____
____
TERMITE
____
TO WALK
WHITE

FENCHEL
BLUMENLADEN
VIERZIG
____
TELLER
TÜMMLER
____
FRÜHLING
TREPPE
GESCHÄFT
BADEANZUG
____
TRINKEN
____
____

RANDOM REVIEW

Random Review: The word list below has been randomly selected from the words covered in this book. Draw lines between the right and left columns to match the words with their translations. Good luck!

A	G	G	T	V	E	G	E	T	A	B	L	E	S	N
N	O	O	P	S	A	E	T	Ü	F	T	L	E	R	H
E	L	H	R	T	C	H	O	S	P	I	T	A	L	A
I	D	E	O	I	A	F	I	T	D	L	T	H	E	B
S	I	G	F	F	L	B	Ü	O	U	I	T	R	T	G
E	U	D	O	F	R	L	C	K	U	L	R	O	U	N
V	Q	E	O	Ü	Ö	O	A	G	R	A	P	K	N	I
E	S	H	K	S	R	L	N	L	T	H	R	S	I	L
N	E	E	H	C	M	E	E	I	L	O	A	T	M	W
T	S	S	U	A	H	G	G	E	K	I	F	T	A	O
E	U	Ü	R	O	O	I	T	O	T	P	R	L	E	B
E	O	M	T	O	T	O	D	V	T	U	M	O	U	B
N	H	E	Z	B	E	I	S	G	R	U	N	U	G	A
E	L	G	N	I	L	W	O	B	N	E	L	I	P	S
S	U	A	H	N	E	K	N	A	R	K	M	P	M	E

BOWLING alley	BOWLINGBAHN
CROCODILE	GEMÜSE
GORILLA	GITARRE
GUITAR	GORILLA
HEDGEHOG	HAUS
HOSPITAL	HOTEL
HOTEL	IGEL
HOUSE	KALMAR
MINUTE	KRANKENHAUS
PLUTO	KROKODIL
PUMPKIN	KÜRBIS
SEVENTEEN	MINUTE
SQUID	PLUTO
TEASPOON	SIEBZEHN
VEGETABLES	TEELÖFFEL

RANDOM REVIEW

134

Random Review: The word list below has been randomly selected from the words covered in this book. Find the missing translations hidden in the wordsearch grid and fill-in-the-blanks in the word list below. Good luck!

E	S	E	U	G	U	T	R	O	P	E	O	S	E	E
P	H	O	A	R	E	E	R	Ä	E	S	A	E	I	R
O	O	C	U	Ä	S	S	L	B	B	U	P	A	E	N
L	N	L	S	R	T	T	Y	W	R	H	M	F	O	E
I	I	I	I	I	C	E	I	E	K	K	C	O	R	T
C	G	R	A	Z	N	R	S	N	L	T	C	S	O	T
E	B	Ä	T	O	E	A	E	I	K	C	O	B	A	T
S	I	G	H	A	H	I	E	A	A	T	U	F	O	W
T	E	R	E	N	M	B	R	R	M	Y	I	T	Q	F
A	N	V	E	I	E	R	N	E	O	S	A	E	G	E
T	E	A	O	N	N	Y	U	E	V	K	K	T	R	E
I	F	H	U	L	A	K	J	R	E	I	T	U	Ü	E
O	W	J	O	M	O	P	U	K	O	R	E	A	N	N
N	E	F	U	A	K	T	N	W	D	T	G	R	S	K
Y	P	O	R	T	U	G	I	E	S	I	S	C	H	E

GREEN ______
HONEYBEE ____________
JUNE _____
KNEE _____
KOREAN _____________
MAY ____
POLICE STATION _______________
PORTUGUESE ________________
RACCOON ___________
SKIRT ______
SKUNK __________
SOUR CREAM _______ ______
TO BUY ________
TO LOVE _______
TO TAKE ________

RANDOM REVIEW

135

Random Review: The word list below has been randomly selected from the words covered in this book. Find the missing translations hidden in the wordsearch grid and fill-in-the-blanks in the word list below. Good luck!

V	S	A	L	A	T	S	C	H	Ü	S	S	E	L	R
T	E	O	D	P	A	W	E	F	I	F	T	Y	K	E
D	E	D	H	L	V	H	E	V	E	M	N	R	C	P
A	S	T	A	I	H	S	G	L	E	U	W	E	E	P
T	T	D	E	Ö	O	I	R	C	V	N	O	N	F	E
S	E	R	S	G	H	F	A	U	I	E	T	H	N	P
N	R	S	N	E	Ü	R	L	H	O	A	N	Y	Ü	D
E	N	O	B	N	C	A	C	T	G	F	W	W	F	E
N	B	F	F	R	T	T	D	O	S	V	O	E	S	R
N	N	Z	N	O	U	S	N	I	C	C	D	O	O	S
I	I	H	U	N	D	B	A	W	H	H	L	E	G	K
G	I	Z	B	E	I	S	U	E	E	C	I	I	N	I
F	L	Ö	W	Z	G	O	D	S	O	E	G	N	O	N
E	V	O	R	O	R	T	E	T	P	E	K	T	B	N
R	O	T	E	R	E	N	E	ß	E	I	L	H	C	S

________	BONGOS
________	FÜNFECK
________	FÜNFZIG
________	HUND
________	INNENSTADT
________	KINN
____ ____	ROTER paprika
______ bowl	SALATSCHÜSSEL
___ ______	SCHLIEßEN
________	SEESTERN
________	SIEBZIG
________	VIER
________	VORORTE
________	WOCHE
________	ZWÖLF

RANDOM REVIEW

136

Random Review: The word list below has been randomly selected from the words covered in this book. Find the missing translations hidden in the wordsearch grid and fill-in-the-blanks in the word list below. Good luck!

B	R	A	U	N	L	L	A	B	T	E	K	S	A	B
A	H	E	W	F	R	E	I	T	A	G	N	N	A	Y
E	G	O	E	N	K	E	L	I	N	E	E	S	D	A
T	R	R	T	T	U	G	R	H	R	L	K	G	N	D
B	R	E	A	E	L	P	P	E	C	E	U	H	K	I
M	A	A	E	N	L	G	E	E	T	I	Ä	T	R	R
M	S	E	G	A	D	B	U	B	N	N	R	S	A	F
A	P	E	N	E	M	D	A	E	G	D	A	T	H	E
K	B	E	P	I	N	L	A	E	Z	L	A	Ö	S	C
Ö	E	H	H	S	L	P	R	U	B	G	O	N	T	O
N	R	A	M	S	I	O	E	E	G	O	U	T	T	M
N	R	F	P	G	H	A	I	G	E	H	T	L	O	B
E	I	I	N	I	L	O	I	V	A	S	T	E	F	H
N	E	H	C	N	I	E	W	H	C	S	R	E	E	M
L	S	T	R	A	U	ß	C	T	O	C	A	R	R	Y

FLUGZEUG
BASKETBALLSPIEL
BRAUN
KAMM
FREITAG
ENKELIN
MEERSCHWEINCHEN

____
____
____
____
HAI
____
____
VIOLINE

____
____
____
____
____
____
____
OSTRICH
PENDANT
RASPBERRIES
SAGE
____
TO BE ABLE TO
TO CARRY
____

RANDOM REVIEW

Random Review: The word list below has been randomly selected from the words covered in this book. Draw lines between the right and left columns to match the words with their translations. Good luck!

G	F	R	A	G	E	N	F	M	R	V	C	T	D	T
U	I	O	E	D	O	M	M	O	K	H	W	I	Y	U
Z	A	D	R	E	S	S	E	R	U	S	I	T	B	A
N	R	E	N	F	C	L	O	R	A	R	D	S	E	R
A	I	L	E	I	O	O	C	M	Ä	U	T	P	H	K
F	H	U	T	O	H	H	A	H	C	B	O	E	R	N
A	P	H	H	S	K	J	N	K	Y	L	S	E	E	E
L	A	C	I	A	A	S	I	H	A	R	N	I	S	N
H	S	S	N	P	T	R	A	R	E	K	O	S	E	H
C	T	S	D	P	C	A	B	O	L	Z	E	V	N	O
S	O	B	I	H	E	E	E	E	T	R	R	T	A	B
D	N	R	E	I	A	T	I	R	D	E	O	E	E	S
A	G	E	D	R	E	D	N	A	I	R	O	K	I	E
U	U	A	R	E	W	R	I	E	B	I	T	E	S	V
R	E	D	N	A	I	R	O	C	Z	U	N	G	E	S

BREAD	BOHNENKRAUT
CHURCH	BROT
CORIANDER	EISBÄR
DRESS	ENTE
DRESSER	FRAGEN
DUCK	HINDI
FOURTEEN	KIRCHE
HINDI	KLEID
PAJAMAS	KOMMODE
POLAR BEAR	KORIANDER
SAPPHIRE	SAPHIR
SAVORY	SCHLAFANZUG
SCHOOL	SCHULE
TO ASK	VIERZEHN
TONGUE	ZUNGE

RANDOM REVIEW

Random Review: The word list below has been randomly selected from the words covered in this book. Find the missing translations hidden in the wordsearch grid and fill-in-the-blanks in the word list below. Good luck!

D	R	E	S	P	I	N	K	L	E	G	A	N	A	M
O	P	A	L	E	S	A	R	L	N	T	O	E	O	O
L	P	R	D	N	C	O	T	U	A	L	C	N	S	O
D	M	E	O	I	P	H	R	L	L	S	H	Ä	Ä	R
F	U	B	L	A	E	P	Z	E	A	E	E	Y	N	G
I	J	M	L	A	S	S	C	I	B	N	U	H	E	N
N	H	E	E	H	T	R	C	Y	G	M	T	R	S	I
S	G	V	C	A	A	L	A	H	F	H	E	I	E	N
T	I	O	L	D	I	D	A	I	E	M	C	V	C	I
E	H	N	I	P	O	T	N	N	M	N	S	L	O	D
R	E	S	P	T	H	N	Ä	I	T	A	S	W	I	N
N	H	E	S	Y	I	T	Z	H	S	I	X	T	Y	M
I	R	E	E	S	L	S	M	R	A	D	K	C	I	D
S	Y	N	H	C	S	I	N	N	I	F	K	L	I	M
L	A	R	G	E	I	N	T	E	S	T	I	N	E	I

ATLANTIC ocean ____________
CELLO ________
DINING ROOM ______________
FINNISH ___________
HIGH JUMP _________________
HYENA _________
LARGE INTESTINE _____________
MILK _______
nail CLIPPERS ___________________
NOVEMBER ______________
OPAL _______
RADISH ________________
SIXTY ___________
TODAY ________
total ECLIPSE totale ______________

RANDOM REVIEW

139

Random Review: The word list below has been randomly selected from the words covered in this book. Find the missing translations hidden in the wordsearch grid and fill-in-the-blanks in the word list below. Good luck!

I	K	T	N	G	R	A	N	D	M	O	T	H	E	R
E	A	S	Ü	ß	Y	E	I	O	H	R	E	O	E	E
C	N	D	H	N	I	H	Z	O	G	A	N	T	B	C
F	I	N	G	E	R	E	N	I	R	E	T	O	A	I
S	N	A	K	G	A	E	ß	T	G	U	H	L	C	F
I	C	S	R	N	Y	I	G	E	M	H	I	L	K	F
S	H	H	I	T	E	I	R	ß	S	E	R	A	Ä	O
T	E	E	W	R	E	H	O	A	H	R	T	B	N	E
E	N	I	D	Ä	Ü	R	O	C	B	Z	Y	ß	E	C
R	S	E	R	R	G	F	I	N	E	B	T	U	K	I
I	O	S	P	E	I	E	E	E	I	A	I	F	C	L
N	C	S	L	N	T	Z	R	A	N	G	N	T	Ü	O
L	C	Ä	G	A	D	R	Z	I	A	R	D	I	R	P
A	E	E	A	D	H	D	A	L	N	E	C	K	A	P
W	R	E	T	M	A	E	B	I	E	Z	I	L	O	P

ARTERIEN ____________
DREIßIG ____________
FINGER ____________
FUßBALL ____________
GROßMUTTER ____________
HALS ____________
HERZ ____________
HONIG ____________
KANINCHEN ____________
KATZE ____________
OZEANIEN ____________
POLIZEIBEAMTER ________ ________
RÜCKEN ____________
SCHWÄGERIN ______-_-____
SPRÜHREGEN ____________

RANDOM REVIEW

140

Random Review: The word list below has been randomly selected from the words covered in this book. Find the missing translations hidden in the wordsearch grid and fill-in-the-blanks in the word list below. Good luck!

```
L K Ü H L S C H R A N K I E A
E B I A R E G I T B O ß I H D
I E O C I A O P O S S U M R R
P K E X V Ü H X S H H L A E A
S C H W E D I S C H R F F S Z
L A B F R N W N I L F R T S I
L J Ü L G H R M L D I I L A L
A M D R A E S A G G E R I W R
B U O L G U B A E M E W A D O
Y S E I S Y E R W W T R S N T
E S T N E R A P I H A R S U I
L O F L E T ß N T N T L M M N
L P L U O N R E T L E U A U O
O O L R J A C K E T T S O A M
V B T H U N D E R S T O R M N
```

____
____
____
____
________ ________
____
OPOSSUM
____
REFRIGERATOR
____
SWEDISH
THUNDERSTORM
TIGER
VOLLEYBALL
____

BLAU
BOXEN
OHR
JACKE
WARAN
MUNDWASSER
____
ELTERN
____
FLUß
____
____
____
____
WAL

RANDOM REVIEW

141

Random Review: The word list below has been randomly selected from the words covered in this book. Draw lines between the right and left columns to match the words with their translations. Good luck!

S	B	U	M	B	L	E	B	E	E	W	E	W	Ö	L
R	B	A	S	E	M	E	N	T	E	S	E	L	E	M
F	N	O	I	L	N	E	T	D	A	I	W	S	A	U
Y	R	C	T	K	F	Y	N	E	ß	S	M	R	A	N
T	E	I	L	L	E	E	R	W	K	I	S	N	E	D
P	T	K	E	E	S	L	A	A	T	C	A	B	E	H
I	I	H	C	D	M	L	L	T	T	N	I	I	A	A
N	R	E	A	O	H	M	W	E	A	E	S	R	R	R
E	W	Y	M	E	H	O	U	S	R	H	M	N	C	M
A	O	A	E	A	C	E	F	H	O	O	H	E	L	O
P	T	D	E	H	R	U	C	C	N	N	L	H	C	N
P	A	N	Z	U	G	S	K	I	O	N	N	D	R	I
L	S	U	I	T	ß	E	C	I	F	L	K	T	B	K
E	E	S	ß	R	Y	A	R	B	E	L	U	G	A	A
F	C	R	I	C	K	E	T	P	L	E	H	O	T	G

BASEMENT
BELUGA
BUMBLEBEE
CEMETARY
CRICKET
HARMONICA
ICE HOCKEY
LION
MARS
PINEAPPLE
SUIT
SUNDAY
TO HELP
TO WRITE
WEDNESDAY

ANANAS
ANZUG
CRICKET
EISHOCKEY
FRIEDHOF
HELFEN
HUMMEL
KELLER
LÖWE
MARS
MITTWOCH
MUNDHARMONIKA
SCHREIBEN
SONNTAG
WEIßWAL

RANDOM REVIEW

142

Random Review: The word list below has been randomly selected from the words covered in this book. Find the missing translations hidden in the wordsearch grid and fill-in-the-blanks in the word list below. Good luck!

T	O	T	I	U	Q	S	O	M	M	U	I	C	C	L
A	G	T	W	C	R	L	T	O	G	A	R	A	G	E
A	A	O	A	A	O	E	S	R	H	L	S	N	T	I
T	R	R	T	P	G	K	N	P	U	A	B	E	U	P
S	A	E	B	R	I	E	F	S	S	M	P	A	B	S
S	G	A	T	T	B	T	N	S	N	M	P	A	H	L
E	E	D	O	R	E	T	A	V	O	S	R	E	I	L
D	H	C	S	I	E	L	F	R	S	C	N	L	T	A
N	O	E	N	N	G	H	T	N	I	N	E	H	S	B
U	M	Y	B	A	S	S	E	I	B	S	O	L	R	R
B	E	G	L	B	D	E	L	L	E	B	I	L	E	E
I	A	L	C	L	A	O	F	N	B	P	C	T	H	S
S	T	A	T	E	U	R	T	N	E	Z	N	A	T	S
O	T	S	S	E	A	M	K	G	U	S	E	A	A	A
N	Y	L	F	N	O	G	A	R	D	O	O	N	F	W

BISON __________
BRIEFS _______
CAR ____________
CRAB ______________
DRAGONFLY _____________
FATHER ___________
GARAGE ______________
GLASS _________
MEAT _____________
MOSQUITO ______________
STATE _______________________
TO DANCE _____________
TO READ __________
TRUMPET _________________
water POLO _____________________________

RANDOM REVIEW

143

Random Review: The word list below has been randomly selected from the words covered in this book. Find the missing translations hidden in the wordsearch grid and fill-in-the-blanks in the word list below. Good luck!

O	S	T	H	L	A	U	N	D	R	Y	R	O	O	M
S	P	I	N	A	T	D	H	E	U	N	I	N	A	U
F	S	C	B	S	E	O	I	T	H	A	H	O	A	H
I	E	U	P	N	I	L	C	E	D	C	S	E	N	R
F	T	B	N	E	E	N	Z	H	A	M	T	G	P	E
I	U	D	R	D	N	I	N	N	A	A	A	I	N	T
S	B	R	N	U	E	G	I	E	N	N	N	P	K	H
C	A	A	N	R	A	P	U	T	T	G	G	E	S	C
H	H	H	D	E	S	R	E	I	U	O	O	E	I	U
C	E	C	E	O	J	L	L	I	N	L	E	K	N	E
D	B	S	S	U	O	O	N	Ä	N	D	E	R	N	L
T	U	S	L	P	P	E	T	H	I	R	T	E	E	N
U	A	I	E	E	Y	R	A	U	R	B	E	F	T	O
C	T	W	E	F	I	S	H	A	K	Ü	C	H	E	R
W	A	S	C	H	K	Ü	C	H	E	Y	L	U	J	K

___ ______ ÄNDERN
________ ANTILOPE
________ DREIZEHN
________ FEBRUAR
________ FISCH
________ JULI
________ KRONLEUCHTER
________ KÜCHE
______ ______ MANGOLD
________ PINGUIN
________ SPINAT
________ TAUBE
________ TENNIS
________ TUBA
________ ______ WASCHKÜCHE

RANDOM REVIEW

144

Random Review: The word list below has been randomly selected from the words covered in this book. Find the missing translations hidden in the wordsearch grid and fill-in-the-blanks in the word list below. Good luck!

P	U	K	C	I	P	O	D	H	I	E	W	P	N	T
N	I	A	R	Y	V	A	E	H	D	I	F	S	A	H
F	E	A	E	R	Y	R	L	F	F	I	R	S	A	R
P	E	I	S	T	A	R	K	E	R	R	E	G	E	N
L	L	T	L	U	A	A	A	S	M	F	L	K	E	A
B	A	A	N	I	A	L	I	U	O	A	H	N	I	E
U	T	A	T	D	T	C	P	H	N	C	K	O	A	C
S	J	U	Ü	E	H	P	N	T	A	A	C	L	S	O
S	E	I	R	E	A	H	E	M	A	N	J	L	P	C
T	I	L	K	K	A	U	E	R	M	G	I	I	I	I
A	G	N	I	B	I	L	O	C	K	E	T	A	C	F
T	H	H	S	T	T	S	F	E	D	D	H	D	K	I
I	T	U	C	A	P	R	H	E	T	T	S	E	U	C
O	B	T	H	C	A	E	P	I	I	R	Y	M	P	A
N	C	O	E	U	P	B	R	K	I	F	I	Z	A	P

____ ________

____
DAY
EIGHT
HAT
HEAVY RAIN
JANUARY

____
PACIFIC OCEAN

____
________ truck
PLATEAU
REPTILES

____
WIFE

BUSBAHNHOF
KAMEL

____

______

____

__________ _______

____
MEDAILLON

____
PFIRSICH
PICKUP

____

____
TÜRKISCH

______

RANDOM REVIEW

Random Review: The word list below has been randomly selected from the words covered in this book. Draw lines between the right and left columns to match the words with their translations. Good luck!

```
K N I E W H C S L E H C A T S
N Ü A E W T W U V Ö G E L B W
E T H C Ü R F I F H W B A I T
L P I L O T I L N O G I N R I
E I N U F N U S B T R T E D C
G T O Ä R G N L T P E E Y S P
D N E S H F E A O R S R D T O
N G I A R A A R M U U N E R R
A I F K C U T D M E O O R U C
H E H E C H T W O M H A E M U
N W M E Ö O E O O T T E R P P
P Z P I L O T R N B R D H F I
E N T D N A B S U H U R E D N
N C R A I N Ä N E G O B L L E
E D U Ä B E G S T H C I R E G
```

AIRPORT	EHEMANN
BIRDS	ELLBOGEN
COURTHOUSE	FLUGHAFEN
ELBOW	FRÜCHTE
FRUIT	GERICHTSGEBÄUDE
HUSBAND	HANDGELENK
MOON	LEHRER
OIL	MOND
PILOT	ÖL
PORCUPINE	PILOT
STOCKING	STACHELSCHWEIN
TEACHER	STRUMPF
TWO	VÖGEL
WINTER	WINTER
WRIST	ZWEI

RANDOM REVIEW

146

Random Review: The word list below has been randomly selected from the words covered in this book. Find the missing translations hidden in the wordsearch grid and fill-in-the-blanks in the word list below. Good luck!

T	E	T	T	E	I	V	R	E	S	S	E	M	A	S
R	G	U	R	L	P	I	P	L	T	H	C	R	I	T
O	U	M	Q	I	F	A	U	C	U	O	C	X	T	R
P	L	F	N	S	R	E	N	N	R	O	D	E	L	O
I	V	K	N	K	O	A	U	U	K	Ä	O	S	S	P
S	O	E	O	O	P	M	H	Ä	E	H	L	N	A	I
C	T	F	R	K	O	A	U	L	Y	A	N	C	L	C
H	L	I	I	K	M	N	L	E	M	M	I	A	T	A
E	A	N	H	S	A	E	K	M	A	S	C	N	S	L
R	H	K	T	O	S	U	A	E	E	T	H	O	R	S
S	W	E	U	O	A	M	F	N	L	E	T	F	E	T
T	R	U	T	H	A	H	N	E	I	R	E	Y	F	O
U	A	D	E	L	A	W	R	A	N	E	T	T	A	R
R	N	A	P	A	R	K	B	E	E	H	C	S	O	M
M	A	S	O	R	S	Ä	U	G	E	T	I	E	R	E

HAMSTER ____________
KNIFE ____________
LUGE ____________
MAMMALS ____________
MOSQUE ____________
NAPKIN ____________
NARWHAL ____________
NIECE ____________
PARK ____________
PINK ____________
SIX ____________
TO SELL ____________
TROPICAL STORM ____________ ______
TURKEY ____________
UNCLE ____________

RANDOM REVIEW

147

Random Review: The word list below has been randomly selected from the words covered in this book. Find the missing translations hidden in the wordsearch grid and fill-in-the-blanks in the word list below. Good luck!

P	O	L	I	Z	E	I	F	A	H	R	Z	E	U	G
L	T	W	R	S	E	N	D	L	E	G	E	I	P	S
A	O	Ä	A	U	E	A	N	M	R	E	F	O	O	R
R	G	E	C	S	C	E	M	A	M	A	L	L	E	T
D	O	B	E	I	C	A	S	O	W	R	Ä	T	N	H
E	C	U	C	D	H	H	D	I	E	E	H	E	R	C
H	B	T	I	Z	A	L	M	L	T	C	D	O	A	A
T	U	T	L	M	N	K	D	A	O	E	F	A	H	D
A	T	O	O	I	E	A	I	T	S	K	E	W	B	N
C	H	C	P	R	H	S	T	Z	O	C	A	E	E	O
C	T	K	T	R	C	R	S	O	I	S	H	H	W	ß
I	A	H	ß	O	U	W	L	B	H	L	E	I	D	Ä
I	B	T	R	R	S	O	H	E	A	G	L	E	N	S
D	A	U	G	H	T	E	R	K	A	N	A	A	N	E
E	R	U	S	A	E	M	E	P	A	T	D	I	I	G

______	ADLER
_________	BADEWANNE
______	DACH
____________	DOM
__ __	GEHEN
_________	GESÄß
_______	HOLZHAMMER
____ ________	MESSBAND
_____ ___	POLIZEIFAHRZEUG
_____	SEE
_______	SPIEGEL
__ ____ ___	SUCHEN
_________	TOCHTER
_______	WASCHMASCHINE
_______	ZIKADE

RANDOM REVIEW

148

Random Review: The word list below has been randomly selected from the words covered in this book. Find the missing translations hidden in the wordsearch grid and fill-in-the-blanks in the word list below. Good luck!

```
Z W V I S C H W E R T W A L S
M U N O P W A T U E S D A Y E
O O C I R A A L T M B S E H I
O N G C E B Z O L M E I L T R
R Z I R H W A L L I G A T O R
G E U O I I H U M Z G T E T E
N T P C N L N C W N N A T O B
I E G I C E S I S H A H T C W
V G R D V H E S S O L F A O A
I N U E N B I D E W R S A O R
L A B R E T D N D T T A O K T
M R A L H B E A I L O T N I S
H O H M C T D I E N S T A G I
S H C R O P P R E P I V G L E
H C A A K I L L E R W H A L E
```

____

ARM

CASTLE

dental ______

KILLER WHALE

______ ______

______

ORANGE

PIG

PORCH

____

___ _____

____

______

ZUCCHINI

ALLIGATOR

_____

_____

ZAHNSEIDE

____

WOHNZIMMER

ZWIEBEL

____

____

______

ERDBEEREN

KOCHEN

DIENSTAG

VIPER

____

RANDOM REVIEW

149

Random Review: The word list below has been randomly selected from the words covered in this book. Draw lines between the right and left columns to match the words with their translations. Good luck!

N	S	R	E	T	A	E	H	T	E	I	V	O	M	A
E	C	V	I	E	D	E	A	G	R	E	I	E	G	S
K	H	S	U	I	Z	R	E	S	O	C	K	S	F	W
C	U	K	O	L	R	S	A	W	E	O	V	T	L	O
O	L	I	Y	A	T	T	A	P	O	L	S	E	O	C
S	D	N	G	R	O	U	B	T	E	O	M	E	H	G
N	E	O	A	W	U	M	R	S	U	G	T	W	Y	A
O	N	G	A	N	E	C	D	E	N	R	W	O	K	T
O	O	N	H	R	D	I	R	L	V	A	N	L	A	T
N	T	R	K	I	N	T	A	E	L	A	G	L	U	I
R	O	U	U	H	P	O	L	L	M	S	A	E	F	M
E	R	T	C	F	L	E	A	W	M	M	O	N	R	H
T	W	A	L	L	A	B	Y	H	A	T	E	E	H	C
F	R	S	L	D	Y	O	B	A	S	F	R	T	O	A
A	E	E	R	E	I	T	N	E	N	N	I	P	S	N

AFTERNOON
ARACHNIDS
CHEETAH
FLEA
GOOSE
MERCURY
MOVIE THEATER
SATURN
SOCKS
TARRAGON
TO OWE
TO WANT
TOE
VULTURE
WALLABY

ESTRAGON
FLOH
GANS
GEIER
GEPARD
KINO
MERKUR
NACHMITTAG
SATURN
SCHULDEN
SOCKEN
SPINNENTIERE
WALLABY
WOLLEN
ZEH

RANDOM REVIEW

150

Random Review: The word list below has been randomly selected from the words covered in this book. Find the missing translations hidden in the wordsearch grid and fill-in-the-blanks in the word list below. Good luck!

E	E	U	T	S	I	N	N	E	T	H	C	S	I	T
R	N	R	O	O	R	R	R	A	H	T	S	H	O	R
U	I	P	H	T	O	A	O	A	T	L	A	S	W	E
T	N	E	A	D	T	B	B	R	S	I	N	N	E	T
A	T	T	V	Ä	Y	E	L	T	L	U	M	N	S	T
R	D	E	E	C	N	A	L	U	B	M	A	E	T	U
E	E	R	M	R	F	U	N	O	E	R	R	E	E	N
P	V	S	A	P	W	D	O	N	I	N	G	W	E	G
M	S	I	W	Z	E	Ä	I	H	O	V	A	O	S	S
E	R	L	O	R	I	R	S	C	Y	A	R	S	H	W
T	O	I	W	L	A	L	A	C	E	E	I	T	C	A
N	U	E	N	G	E	T	E	T	H	I	N	O	E	G
E	A	D	R	I	S	T	C	Ä	U	E	E	B	D	E
R	H	A	G	E	L	Y	E	L	S	R	A	P	I	N
H	M	K	V	S	A	L	Z	S	T	R	E	U	E	R

AMBULANCE ____________________
BAR _____
BOAT ______
HAIL ________
LIZARD ___________
MARGARINE _____________
NINE ______
PARSLEY ____________
SALT shaker ________________
table TENNIS ______________
TEMPERATURE _______________
TO HAVE ________
UNDERWEAR _________________
VEST ________
VIOLET _________

SOLUTIONS

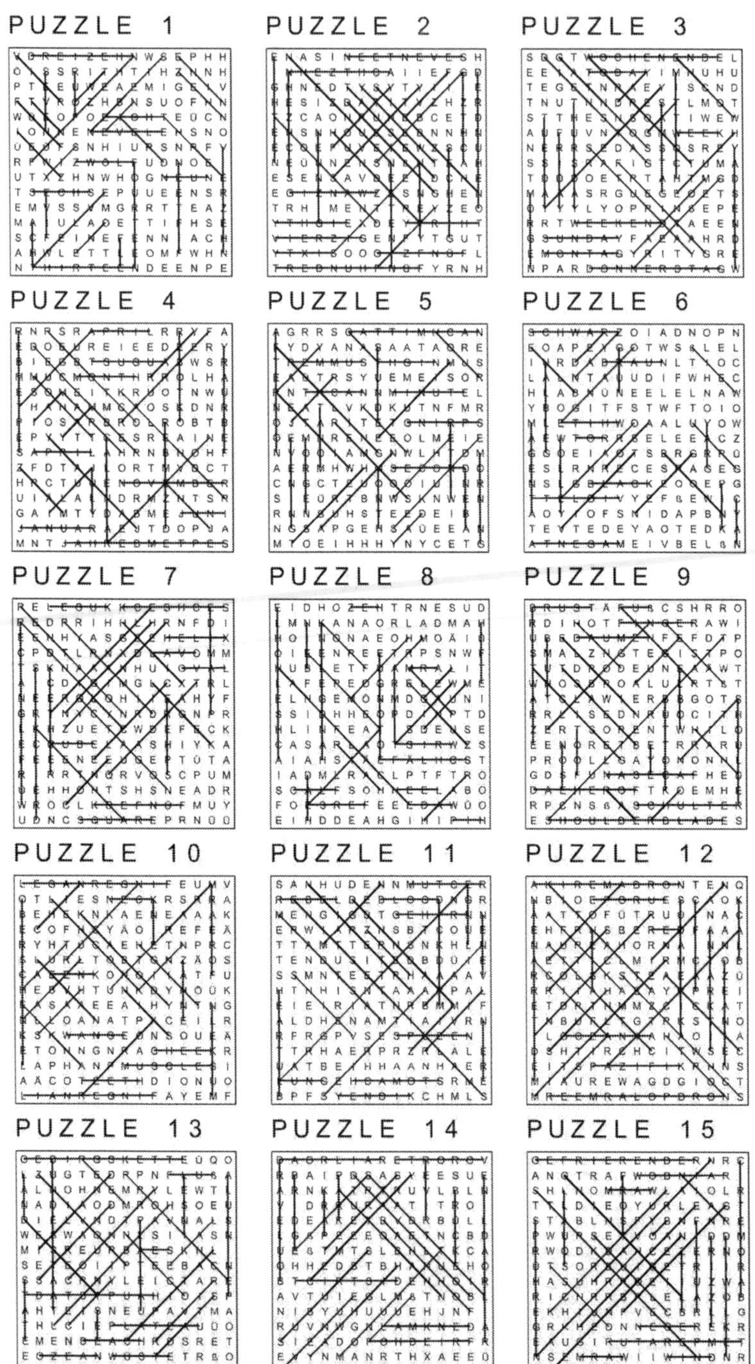
PUZZLE 1
PUZZLE 2
PUZZLE 3
PUZZLE 4
PUZZLE 5
PUZZLE 6
PUZZLE 7
PUZZLE 8
PUZZLE 9
PUZZLE 10
PUZZLE 11
PUZZLE 12
PUZZLE 13
PUZZLE 14
PUZZLE 15

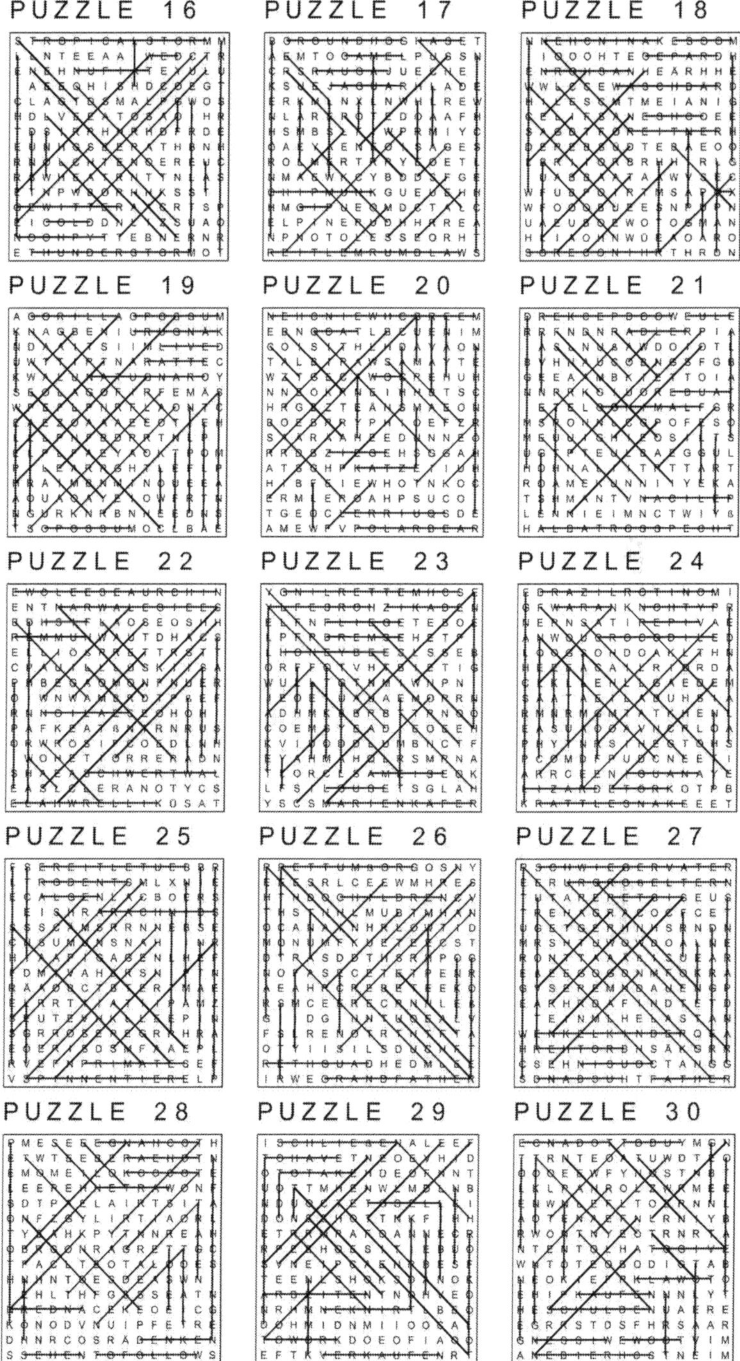
PUZZLE 16
PUZZLE 17
PUZZLE 18
PUZZLE 19
PUZZLE 20
PUZZLE 21
PUZZLE 22
PUZZLE 23
PUZZLE 24
PUZZLE 25
PUZZLE 26
PUZZLE 27
PUZZLE 28
PUZZLE 29
PUZZLE 30

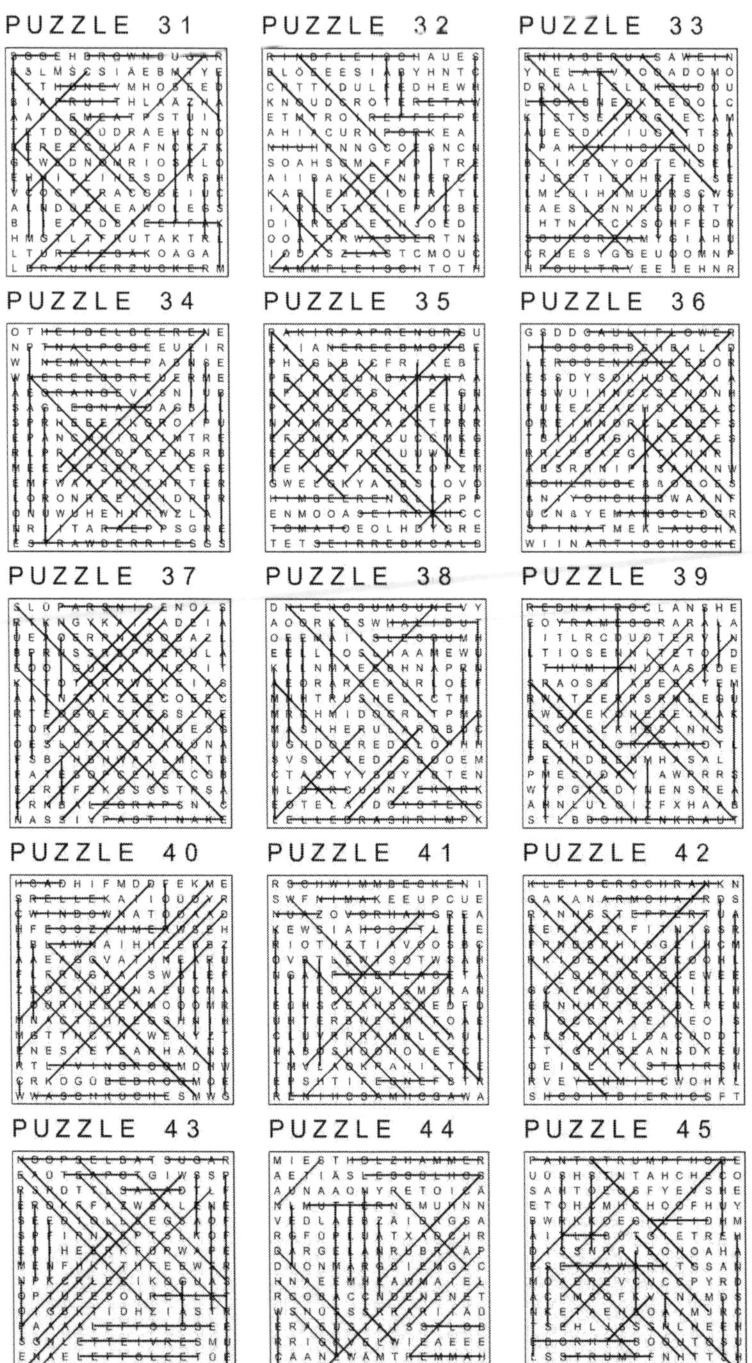

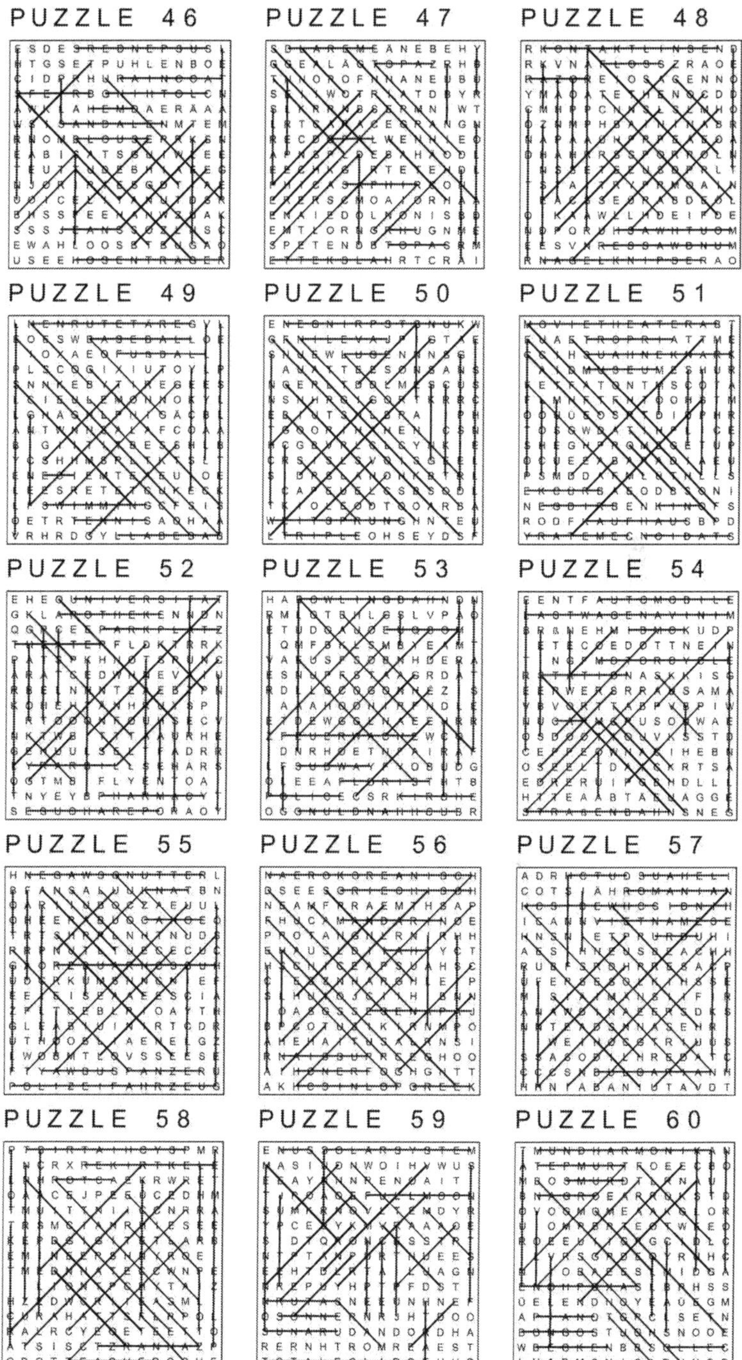
PUZZLE 46
PUZZLE 47
PUZZLE 48
PUZZLE 49
PUZZLE 50
PUZZLE 51
PUZZLE 52
PUZZLE 53
PUZZLE 54
PUZZLE 55
PUZZLE 56
PUZZLE 57
PUZZLE 58
PUZZLE 59
PUZZLE 60

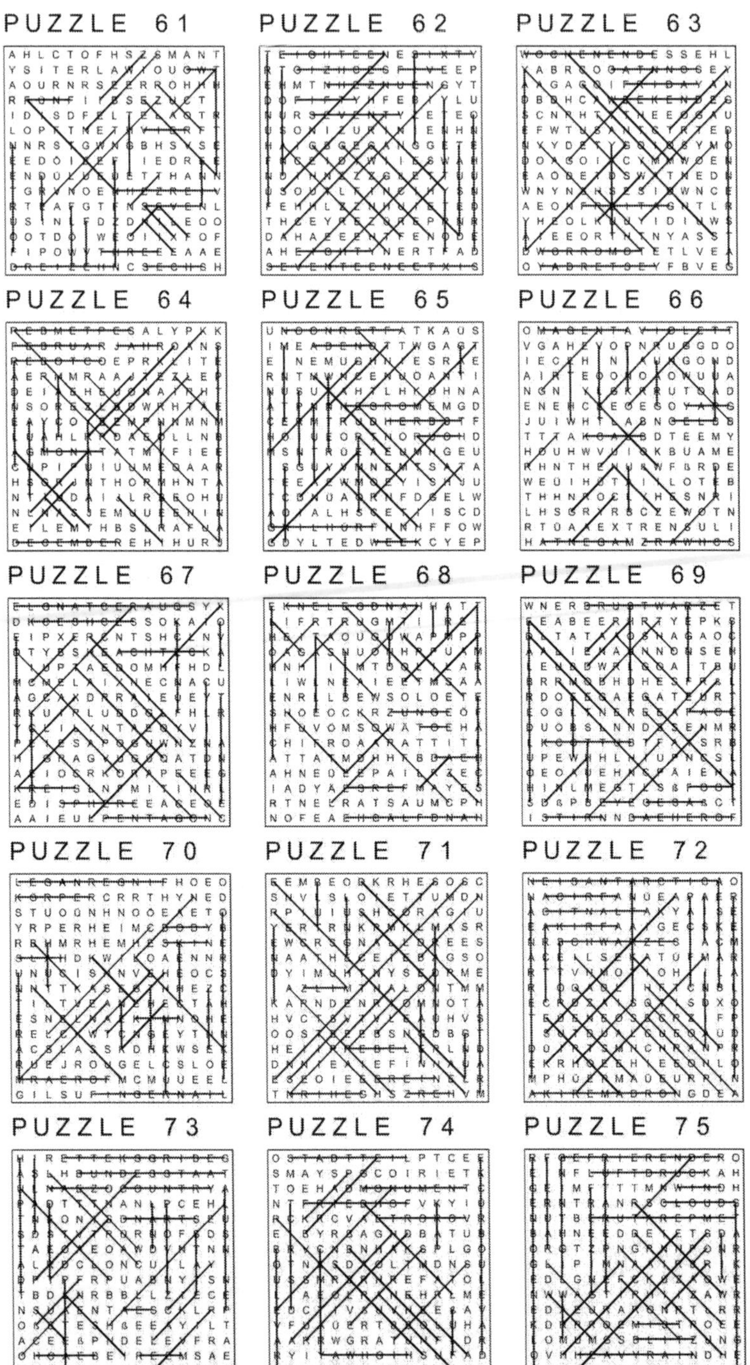
PUZZLE 61
PUZZLE 62
PUZZLE 63
PUZZLE 64
PUZZLE 65
PUZZLE 66
PUZZLE 67
PUZZLE 68
PUZZLE 69
PUZZLE 70
PUZZLE 71
PUZZLE 72
PUZZLE 73
PUZZLE 74
PUZZLE 75

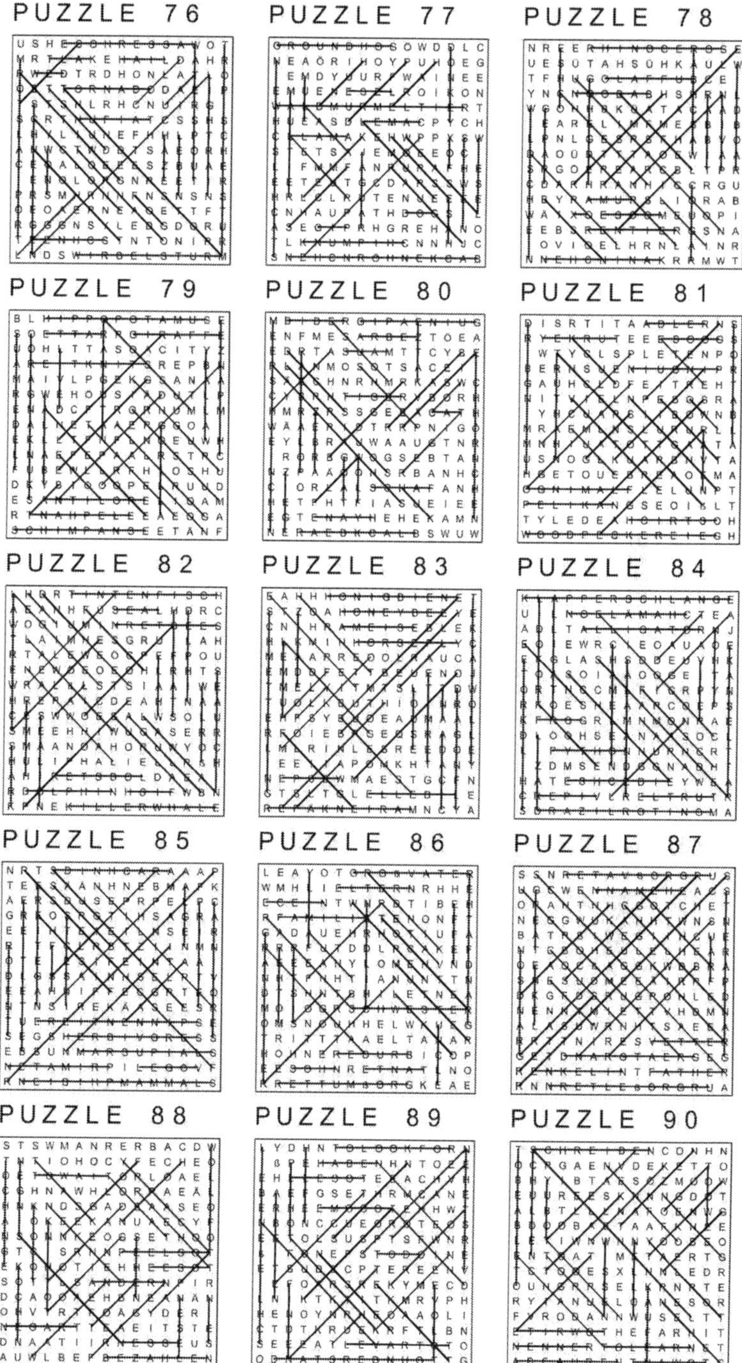

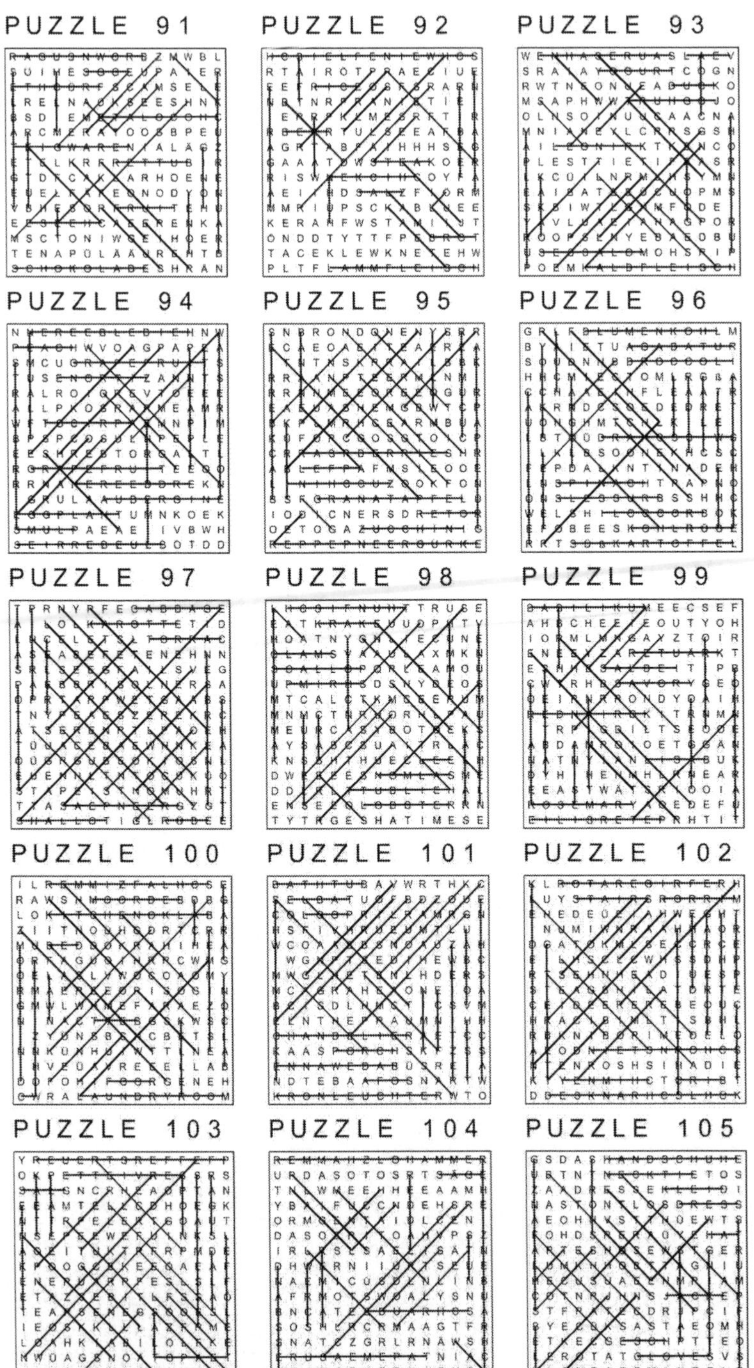

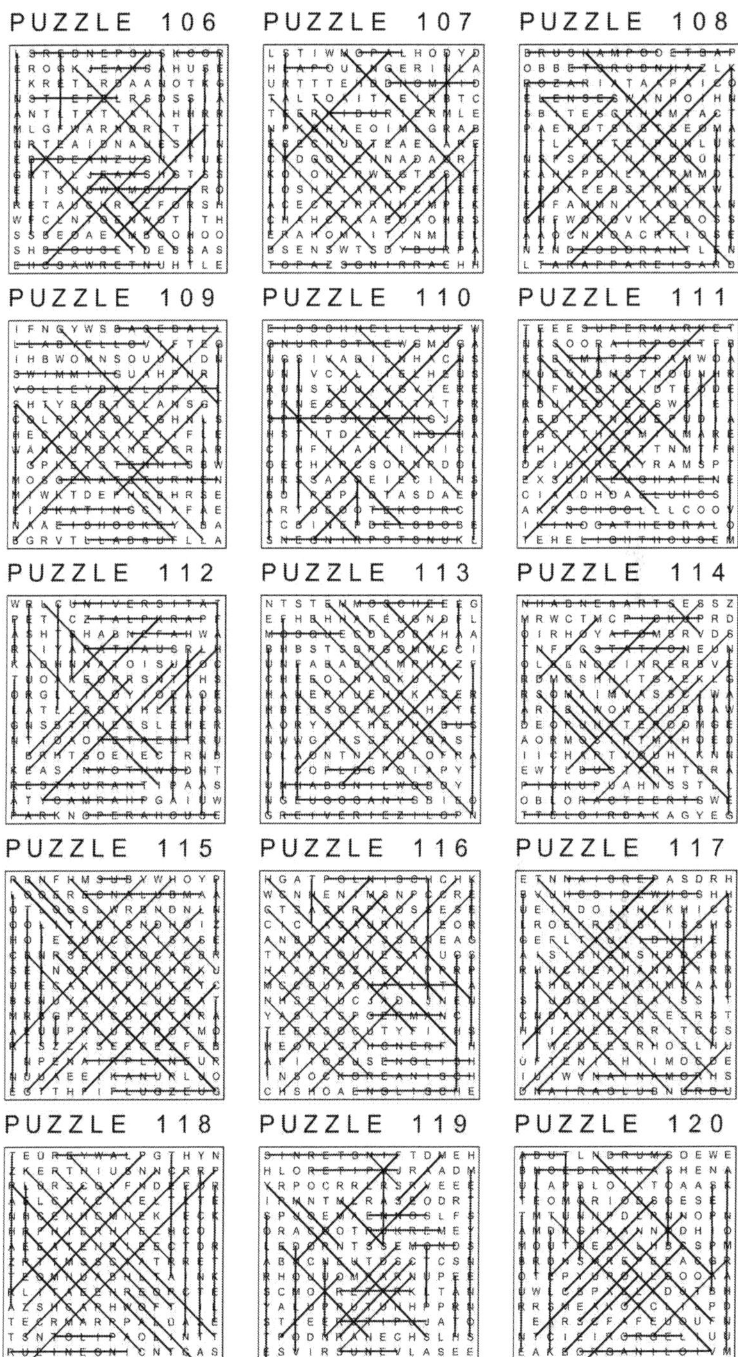
PUZZLE 106
PUZZLE 107
PUZZLE 108
PUZZLE 109
PUZZLE 110
PUZZLE 111
PUZZLE 112
PUZZLE 113
PUZZLE 114
PUZZLE 115
PUZZLE 116
PUZZLE 117
PUZZLE 118
PUZZLE 119
PUZZLE 120

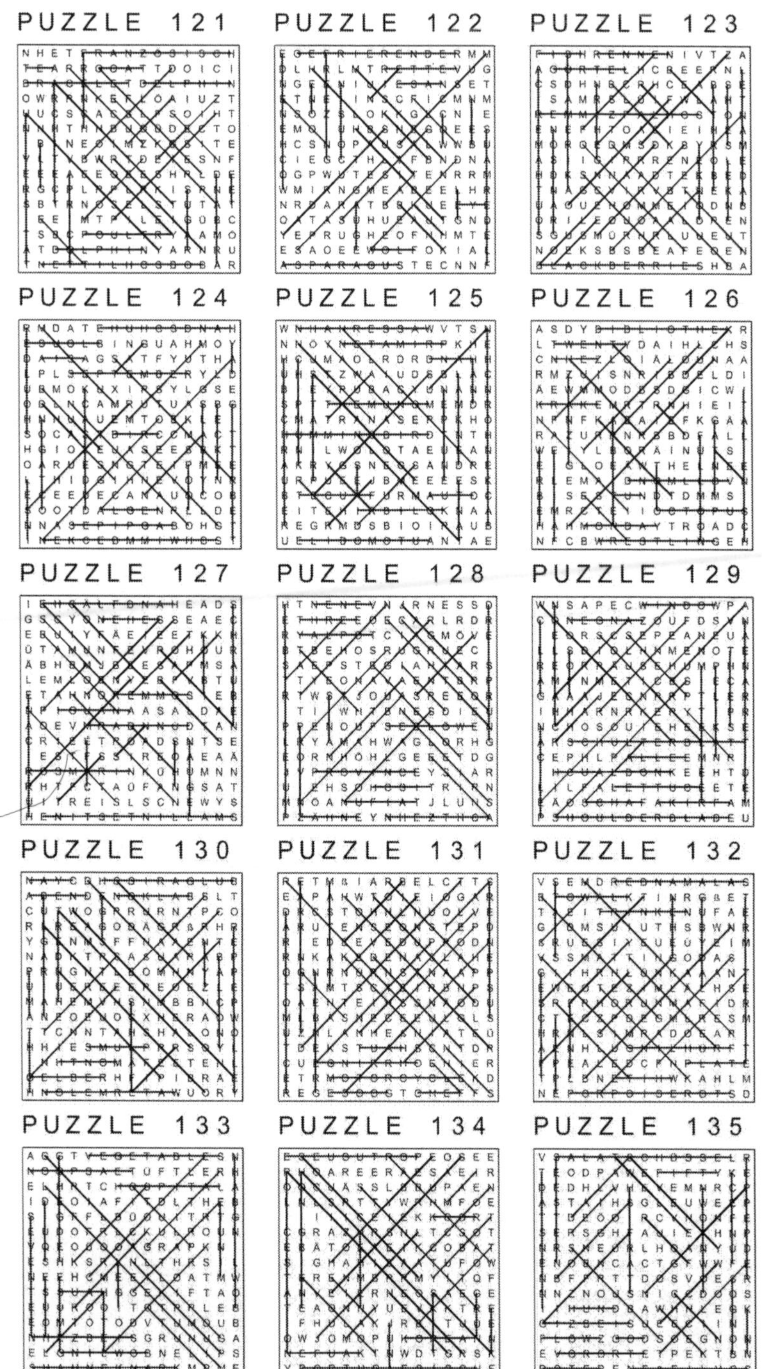
PUZZLE 121
PUZZLE 122
PUZZLE 123
PUZZLE 124
PUZZLE 125
PUZZLE 126
PUZZLE 127
PUZZLE 128
PUZZLE 129
PUZZLE 130
PUZZLE 131
PUZZLE 132
PUZZLE 133
PUZZLE 134
PUZZLE 135

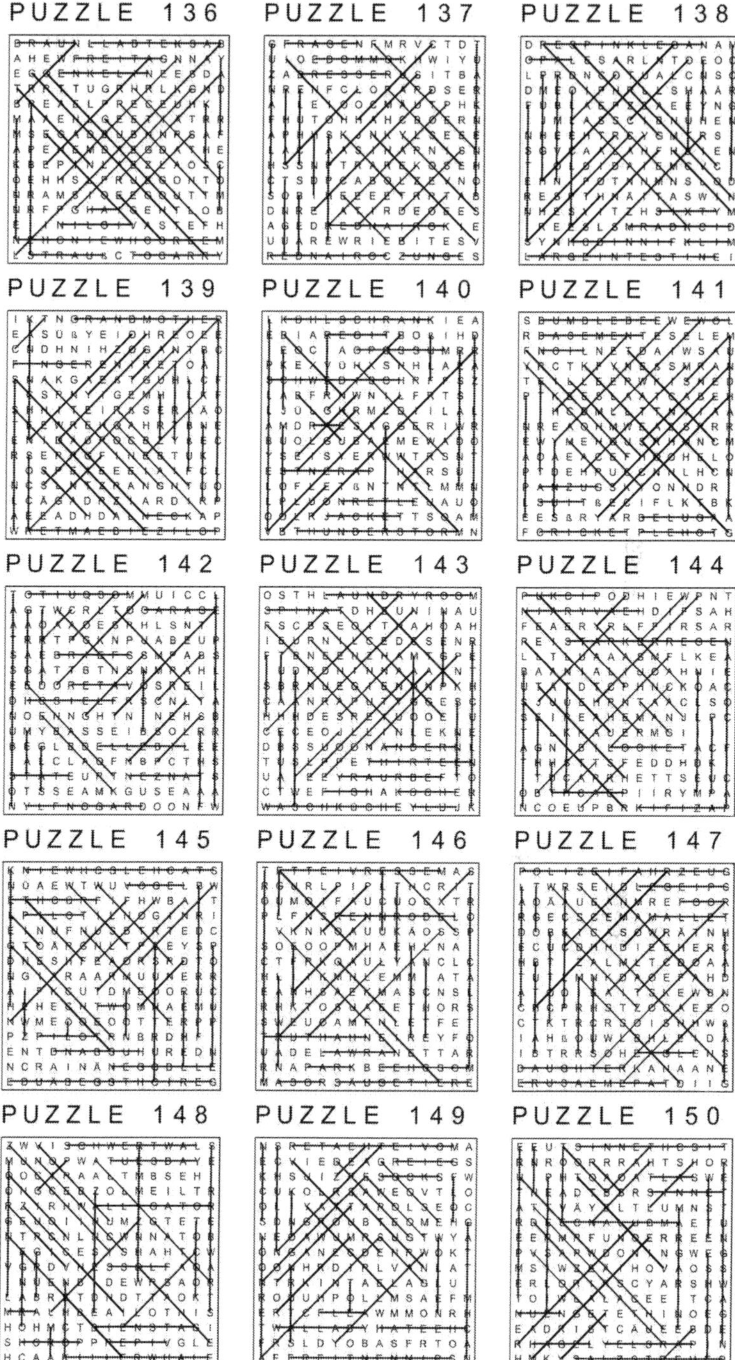
PUZZLE 136
PUZZLE 137
PUZZLE 138
PUZZLE 139
PUZZLE 140
PUZZLE 141
PUZZLE 142
PUZZLE 143
PUZZLE 144
PUZZLE 145
PUZZLE 146
PUZZLE 147
PUZZLE 148
PUZZLE 149
PUZZLE 150

PUZZLE 61

1. EIGHT ACHT
2. ELEVEN ELF
3. FIFTEEN FÜNFZEHN
4. FIVE FÜNF
5. FOUR VIER
6. FOURTEEN VIERZEHN
7. NINE NEUN
8. ONE EIN
9. SEVEN SIEBEN
10. SIX SECHS
11. TEN ZEHN
12. THIRTEEN DREIZEHN
13. THREE DREI
14. TWELVE ZWÖLF
15. TWO ZWEI

PUZZLE 62

1. EIGHTEEN ACHTZEHN
2. EIGHTY ACHTZIG
3. FIFTY FÜNFZIG
4. FIVE HUNDRED FÜNFHUNDERT
5. FORTY VIERZIG
6. NINETEEN NEUNZEHN
7. NINETY NEUNZIG
8. ONE HUNDRED HUNDERT
9. SEVENTEEN SIEBZEHN
10. SEVENTY SIEBZIG
11. SIXTEEN SECHZEHN
12. SIXTY SECHZIG
13. THIRTY DREIßIG
14. THOUSAND TAUSEND
15. TWENTY ZWANZIG

PUZZLE 63

1. TUESDAY DIENSTAG
2. THURSDAY DONNERSTAG
3. FRIDAY FREITAG
4. YESTERDAY GESTERN
5. TODAY HEUTE
6. WEDNESDAY MITTWOCH
7. MONDAY MONTAG
8. TOMORROW MORGEN
9. SATURDAY SAMSTAG
10. SUNDAY SONNTAG
11. DAY TAG
12. WEEK WOCHE
13. WEEKEND WOCHENENDE

PUZZLE 64

1. APRIL APRIL
2. AUGUST AUGUST
3. CALENDAR KALENDER
4. DECEMBER DEZEMBER
5. FEBRUARY FEBRUAR
6. JANUARY JANUAR
7. JULY JULI
8. JUNE JUNI
9. MARCH MÄRZ
10. MAY MAI
11. MONTH MONAT
12. NOVEMBER NOVEMBER
13. OCTOBER OKTOBER
14. SEPTEMBER SEPTEMBER
15. YEAR JAHR

PUZZLE 65

1. AFTERNOON NACHMITTAG
2. AUTUMN HERBST
3. DAY TAG
4. EVENING ABEND
5. HOUR STUNDE
6. MINUTE MINUTE
7. MONTH MONAT
8. MORNING MORGEN
9. NIGHT NACHT
10. SECOND SEKUNDE
11. SPRING FRÜHLING
12. SUMMER SOMMER
13. WEEK WOCHE
14. WINTER WINTER
15. YEAR JAHR

PUZZLE 66

1. BLACK SCHWARZ
2. BLUE BLAU
3. BROWN BRAUN
4. CYAN ZYAN
5. GRAY GRAU
6. GREEN GRÜN
7. MAGENTA MAGENTA
8. ORANGE ORANGE
9. PINK ROSA
10. RED ROT
11. VIOLET VIOLETT
12. WHITE WEIß
13. YELLOW GELB

PUZZLE 67

1. OCTAGON ACHTECK
2. TRIANGLE DREIECK
3. PENTAGON FÜNFECK
4. HELIX HELIX
5. CONE KEGEL
6. CIRCLE KREIS
7. SPHERE KUGEL
8. OVAL OVAL
9. PYRAMID PYRAMIDE
10. SQUARE QUADRAT
11. RECTANGLE RECHTECK
12. HEXAGON SECHSECK
13. CUBE WÜRFEL
14. CYLINDER ZYLINDER

PUZZLE 68

1. ARM ARM
2. ARMPIT ACHSELHÖHLE
3. CALF WADE
4. HAIR HAAR
5. HEAD KOPF
6. HEEL FERSE
7. HIP HÜFTE
8. LEG BEIN
9. MOUTH MUND
10. PALM HANDFLÄCHE
11. TEMPLE SCHLÄFE
12. TOE ZEH
13. TONGUE ZUNGE
14. WAIST TAILLE
15. WRIST HANDGELENK

PUZZLE 69

1. BREAST BRUST
2. BUTTOCK GESÄß
3. EAR OHR
4. ELBOW ELLBOGEN
5. EYE AUGE
6. FACE GESICHT
7. FINGER FINGER
8. FOOT FUß
9. FOREHEAD STIRN
10. HAND HAND
11. NIPPLE BRUSTWARZE
12. NOSE NASE
13. SHOULDER SCHULTER
14. SHOULDER BLADE SCHULTERBLATT
15. THUMB DAUMEN

PUZZLE 70

1. ANKLE KNÖCHEL
2. BACK RÜCKEN
3. BODY KÖRPER
4. CHEEK WANGE
5. CHIN KINN
6. FINGERNAIL FINGERNAGEL
7. FOREARM UNTERARM
8. KNEE KNIE
9. MUSCLES MUSKELN
10. NAVEL NABEL
11. NECK HALS
12. SKIN HAUT
13. TEETH ZÄHNE
14. THIGH OBERSCHENKEL

PUZZLE 71

1. ARTERIES ARTERIEN
2. BLOOD BLUT
3. LARGE INTESTINE DICKDARM
4. SMALL INTESTINE DÜNNDARM
5. BRAIN GEHIRN
6. HEART HERZ
7. LIVER LEBER
8. LUNG LUNGE
9. STOMACH MAGEN
10. RECTUM MASTDARM
11. SPLEEN MILZ
12. KIDNEY NIERE
13. VEINS VENEN

PUZZLE 72

1. AFRICA AFRIKA
2. ANTARCTICA ANTARKTIS
3. ARCTIC OCEAN NORDPOLARMEER
4. ASIA ASIEN
5. ATLANTIC OCEAN ATLANTIK
6. BLACK SEA SCHWARZES MEER
7. EUROPE EUROPA
8. INDIAN OCEAN INDISCHER OZEAN
9. MEDITERRANEAN SEA MITTELMEER
10. NORTH AMERICA NORDAMERIKA
11. OCEANIA OZEANIEN
12. PACIFIC OCEAN PAZIFIK
13. RED SEA ROTES MEER
14. SOUTH AMERICA SÜDAMERIKA

PUZZLE 73

1. BEACH STRAND
2. CAPITAL HAUPTSTADT
3. CITY STADT
4. COUNTRY LAND
5. DESERT WÜSTE
6. ISLAND INSEL
7. LAKE SEE
8. MOUNTAIN RANGE GEBIRGSKETTE
9. OCEAN OZEAN
10. PENINSULA HALBINSEL
11. PLATEAU PLATEAU
12. PROVINCE PROVINZ
13. RIVER FLUß
14. SEA MEER
15. STATE BUNDESSTAAT

PUZZLE 74

1. AVENUE ALLEE
2. BOULEVARD BOULEVARD
3. BRIDGE BRÜCKE
4. CEMETARY FRIEDHOF
5. DISTRICT STADTTEIL
6. HIGHWAY AUTOBAHN
7. MONUMENT DENKMAL
8. PARK PARK
9. RAILROAD LINE EISENBAHN
10. RAILROAD STATION BAHNHOF
11. RIVER FLUß
12. STREET STRAßE
13. SUBURBS VORORTE

PUZZLE 75

1. LIGHTNING BLITZ
2. SQUALL BÖ
3. MIST DUNST
4. FREEZING RAIN GEFRIERENDER REGEN
5. HURRICANE HURRIKAN
6. BAROMETRIC PRESSURE LUFTDRUCK
7. FROST RAUREIF
8. RAIN REGEN
9. RAINBOW REGENBOGEN
10. DRIZZLE SPRÜHREGEN
11. HEAVY RAIN STARKER REGEN
12. TEMPERATURE TEMPERATUR
13. WARM WARM
14. WIND WIND
15. CLOUDS WOLKEN

PUZZLE 76

1. COLD KALT
2. CYCLONE WIRBELSTURM
3. DEW TAU
4. FOG NEBEL
5. HAIL HAGEL
6. HAZE DUNST
7. LIGHT RAIN LEICHTER REGEN
8. SLEET SCHNEEREGEN
9. SNOW SCHNEE
10. THUNDERSTORM GEWITTER
11. TORNADO TORNADO
12. TROPICAL STORM TROPISCHER STURM
13. TYPHOON TAIFUN
14. WATERSPOUT WASSERHOSE

PUZZLE 77

1. CAMEL KAMEL
2. CHIPMUNK BACKENHÖRNCHEN
3. DOG HUND
4. DONKEY ESEL
5. FOX FUCHS
6. GROUNDHOG WALDMURMELTIER
7. HARE HASE
8. HORSE PFERD
9. JAGUAR JAGUAR
10. LEMUR LEMURE
11. LLAMA LAMA
12. MULE MAULTIER
13. PIG SCHWEIN
14. PORCUPINE STACHELSCHWEIN
15. WEASEL WIESEL

PUZZLE 78

1. BABOON PAVIAN
2. BISON BISON
3. BUFFALO BÜFFEL
4. CARIBOU RENTIER
5. CHEETAH GEPARD
6. COUGAR PUMA
7. HAMSTER HAMSTER
8. HEDGEHOG IGEL
9. LEOPARD LEOPARD
10. MOOSE ELCH
11. OX OCHSE
12. RABBIT KANINCHEN
13. RACCOON WASCHBÄR
14. RHINOCEROS NASHORN
15. WILD BOAR WILDSCHWEIN

PUZZLE 79

1. ANTELOPE ANTILOPE
2. ELEPHANT ELEFANT
3. BAT FLEDERMAUS
4. GIRAFFE GIRAFFE
5. GORILLA GORILLA
6. KANGAROO KÄNGURU
7. LION LÖWE
8. HIPPOPOTAMUS NILPFERD
9. OPOSSUM OPOSSUM
10. ORANGUTAN ORANG-UTAN
11. RAT RATTE
12. CHIMPANZEE SCHIMPANSE
13. SKUNK STINKTIER
14. TASMANIAN DEVIL TASMANISCHER TEUFEL
15. WALLABY WALLABY

PUZZLE 80

1. BADGER DACHS
2. BEAVER BIBER
3. BLACK BEAR SCHWARZBÄR
4. CAT KATZE
5. COW KUH
6. MOUSE MAUS
7. GOAT ZIEGE
8. GUINEA PIG MEERSCHWEINCHEN
9. HYENA HYÄNE
10. POLAR BEAR EISBÄR
11. SHEEP SCHAF
12. SQUIRREL EICHHÖRNCHEN
13. TIGER TIGER
14. WOLF WOLF
15. ZEBRA ZEBRA

PUZZLE 81

1. ALBATROSS ALBATROS
2. DUCK ENTE
3. EAGLE ADLER
4. FLAMINGO FLAMINGO
5. GOOSE GANS
6. HUMMINGBIRD KOLIBRI
7. OSTRICH STRAUß
8. OWL EULE
9. PELICAN PELIKAN
10. PENGUIN PINGUIN
11. PIGEON TAUBE
12. RAVEN RABE
13. TURKEY TRUTHAHN
14. VULTURE GEIER
15. WOODPECKER SPECHT

PUZZLE 82

1. BELUGA WEIßWAL
2. DOLPHIN DELPHIN
3. FISH FISCH
4. KILLER WHALE SCHWERTWAL
5. LOBSTER HUMMER
6. NARWHAL NARWAL
7. OCTOPUS TINTENFISCH
8. PORPOISE TÜMMLER
9. SEA LION SEELÖWE
10. SEA URCHIN SEEIGEL
11. SEAL SEEHUND
12. SHARK HAI
13. STARFISH SEESTERN
14. WALRUS WALROß
15. WHALE WAL

PUZZLE 83

1. ANT AMEISE
2. HORSEFLY BREMSE
3. FLY FLIEGE
4. FLEA FLOH
5. HONEYBEE HONIGBIENE
6. HORNET HORNISSE
7. BUMBLEBEE HUMMEL
8. LOUSE LAUS
9. DRAGONFLY LIBELLE
10. LADYBUG MARIENKÄFER
11. MOSQUITO MOSKITO
12. BUTTERFLY SCHMETTERLING
13. TERMITE TERMITE
14. YELLOWJACKET WESPE
15. CICADA ZIKADE

PUZZLE 84

1. ALLIGATOR ALLIGATOR
2. CHAMELEON CHAMÄLEON
3. CROCODILE KROKODIL
4. FROG FROSCH
5. IGUANA LEGUAN
6. LIZARD EIDECHSE
7. MONITOR LIZARD WARAN
8. PYTHON PYTHON
9. RATTLESNAKE KLAPPERSCHLANGE
10. SALAMANDER SALAMANDER
11. SNAKE SCHLANGE
12. TOAD KRÖTE
13. TURTLE SCHILDKRÖTE
14. VIPER VIPER

PUZZLE 85

1. ALGAE ALGEN
2. AMPHIBIANS AMPHIBIEN
3. ARACHNIDS SPINNENTIERE
4. BIRDS VÖGEL
5. CARNIVORES FLEISCHFRESSER
6. FISH FISCH
7. HERBIVORES PFLANZENFRESSER
8. INSECTS INSEKTEN
9. MAMMALS SÄUGETIERE
10. MARSUPIALS BEUTELTIERE
11. PRIMATES PRIMATEN
12. REPTILES REPTILIEN
13. RODENTS NAGETIERE

PUZZLE 86

1. AUNT TANTE
2. BROTHER BRUDER
3. CHILDREN KINDER
4. DAUGHTER TOCHTER
5. FAMILY FAMILIE
6. FATHER VATER
7. GRANDFATHER GROßVATER
8. GRANDMOTHER GROßMUTTER
9. MOTHER MUTTER
10. NEPHEW NEFFE
11. NIECE NICHTE
12. PARENTS ELTERN
13. SISTER SCHWESTER
14. SON SOHN
15. UNCLE ONKEL

PUZZLE 87

1. HUSBAND EHEMANN
2. GRANDSON ENKEL
3. GRANDDAUGHTER ENKELIN
4. GRANDCHILDREN ENKELKINDER
5. WIFE FRAU
6. BROTHER-IN-LAW SCHWAGER
7. SISTER-IN-LAW SCHWÄGERIN
8. MOTHER-IN-LAW SCHWIEGERMUTTER
9. FATHER-IN-LAW SCHWIEGERVATER
10. GREAT GRANDPARENTS URGROßELTERN
11. GREAT GRANDMOTHER URGROßMUTTER
12. GREAT GRANDFATHER URGROßVATER
13. COUSIN VETTER

PUZZLE 88

1. TO ASK FRAGEN
2. TO BE SEIN
3. TO CARRY TRAGEN
4. TO CHANGE ÄNDERN
5. TO COOK KOCHEN
6. TO EAT ESSEN
7. TO FOLLOW FOLGEN
8. TO HEAR HÖREN
9. TO PAY BEZAHLEN
10. TO READ LESEN
11. TO SEE SEHEN
12. TO SING SINGEN
13. TO SLEEP SCHLAFEN
14. TO THINK DENKEN
15. TO WAIT WARTEN

PUZZLE 89

1. TO CLOSE SCHLIEßEN
2. TO COME KOMMEN
3. TO DO TUN
4. TO DRINK TRINKEN
5. TO FIND FINDEN
6. TO HAVE HABEN
7. TO HELP HELFEN
8. TO LOOK FOR SUCHEN
9. TO LOVE LIEBEN
10. TO SELL VERKAUFEN
11. TO SPEAK SPRECHEN
12. TO TAKE NEHMEN
13. TO TRAVEL REISEN
14. TO UNDERSTAND VERSTEHEN
15. TO WORK ARBEITEN

PUZZLE 90

1. TO BE ABLE TO KÖNNEN
2. TO BUY KAUFEN
3. TO DANCE TANZEN
4. TO GIVE GEBEN
5. TO GO GEHEN
6. TO KNOW WISSEN
7. TO LEARN LERNEN
8. TO LEAVE ABFAHREN
9. TO OPEN ÖFFNEN
10. TO OWE SCHULDEN
11. TO PLAY SPIELEN
12. TO RUN RENNEN
13. TO WALK GEHEN
14. TO WANT WOLLEN
15. TO WRITE SCHREIBEN

PUZZLE 91

1. BROWN SUGAR BRAUNER ZUCKER
2. BUTTER BUTTER
3. EGGS EIER
4. MEAT FLEISCH
5. FRUIT FRÜCHTE
6. VEGETABLES GEMÜSE
7. HONEY HONIG
8. COFFEE KAFFEE
9. CHEESE KÄSE
10. FLOUR MEHL
11. MILK MILCH
12. CHOCOLATE SCHOKOLADE
13. TEA TEE
14. PASTA TEIGWAREN
15. SUGAR ZUCKER

PUZZLE 92

1. BEEF RINDFLEISCH
2. BEER BIER
3. BREAD BROT
4. CHICKEN HUHN
5. JUICE SAFT
6. LAMB LAMMFLEISCH
7. MARGARINE MARGARINE
8. OIL ÖL
9. PEPPER PFEFFER
10. PORK SCHWEINEFLEISCH
11. RICE REIS
12. SALT SALZ
13. STEAK STEAK
14. WATER WASSER

PUZZLE 93

1. BAGEL KRINGEL
2. COCOA KAKAO
3. CREAM SAHNE
4. DUCK ENTE
5. GOOSE GANS
6. MAPLE SYRUP AHORNSIRUP
7. MOLASSES MELASSE
8. POULTRY GEFLÜGEL
9. RABBIT KANINCHEN
10. SOUR CREAM SAURE SAHNE
11. TURKEY TRUTHAHN
12. VEAL KALBFLEISCH
13. YOGURT JOGHURT
14. WINE WEIN

PUZZLE 94

1. APRICOT APRIKOSE
2. BLUEBERRIES HEIDELBEEREN
3. EGGPLANT AUBERGINE
4. GRAPEFRUIT GRAPEFRUIT
5. GRAPES WEINTRAUBEN
6. LEMON ZITRONE
7. LIME LIMETTE
8. ORANGE ORANGE
9. PEACH PFIRSICH
10. PEAR BIRNE
11. PINEAPPLE ANANAS
12. PLUMS PFLAUMEN
13. STRAWBERRIES ERDBEEREN
14. WATERMELON WASSERMELONE

PUZZLE 95

1. APPLE APFEL
2. BANANA BANANE
3. BLACKBERRIES BROMBEEREN
4. FIG FEIGE
5. YELLOW PEPPER GELBER PAPRIKA
6. POMEGRANATE GRANATAPFEL
7. GREEN PEPPER GRÜNER PAPRIKA
8. CUCUMBER GURKE
9. RASPBERRIES HIMBEEREN
10. CHERRIES KIRSCHEN
11. PUMPKIN KÜRBIS
12. RED PEPPER ROTER PAPRIKA
13. TOMATO TOMATE
14. ZUCCHINI ZUCCHINI

PUZZLE 96

1. ARTICHOKE ARTISCHOCKE
2. BOK CHOY PAK-CHOI
3. BROCCOLI BROCCOLI
4. BRUSSELS SPROUTS ROSENKOHL
5. CAULIFLOWER BLUMENKOHL
6. FENNEL FENCHEL
7. GARLIC KNOBLAUCH
8. GREEN BEAN GRÜNE BOHNE
9. LEEKS LAUCH
10. RADISH RADIESCHEN
11. RUTABAGA KOHLRÜBE
12. SPINACH SPINAT
13. SWEET POTATO SÜßKARTOFFEL
14. SWISS CHARD MANGOLD

PUZZLE 97

1. ASPARAGUS SPARGEL
2. BEET ROTE BEETE
3. CABBAGE KOHL
4. CARROT KAROTTE
5. CELERY STANGENSELLERIE
6. GREEN PEAS GRÜNE ERBSEN
7. LETTUCE SALAT
8. ONION ZWIEBEL
9. PARSNIP PASTINAKE
10. POTATOES KARTOFFELN
11. SHALLOT SCHALOTTE
12. SNOW PEAS ZUCKERERBSEN
13. TURNIP RÜBE
14. VEGETABLES GEMÜSE

PUZZLE 98

1. ANCHOVY SARDELLE
2. CLAMS VENUSMUSCHELN
3. CRAB KRABBE
4. EEL AAL
5. HALIBUT HEILBUTT
6. LOBSTER HUMMER
7. MUSSELS MUSCHELN
8. OCTOPUS TINTENFISCH
9. OYSTERS AUSTER
10. SALMON LACHS
11. SCALLOP KAMMMUSCHEL
12. SHRIMP GARNELE
13. SOLE SCHOLLE
14. SQUID KALMAR
15. TUNA THUNFISCH

PUZZLE 99

1. ANISE ANIS
2. BASIL BASILIKUM
3. SAVORY BOHNENKRAUT
4. DILL DILL
5. TARRAGON ESTRAGON
6. CORIANDER KORIANDER
7. HERBS KRÄUTER
8. SWEET BAY LORBEER
9. MINT MINZE
10. OREGANO ORIGANO
11. PARSLEY PETERSILIE
12. ROSEMARY ROSMARIN
13. SAGE SALBEI
14. THYME THYMIAN

PUZZLE 100

1. BALCONY BALKON
2. BASEMENT KELLER
3. BATHROOM WC
4. BED BETT
5. BEDROOM SCHLAFZIMMER
6. DINING ROOM ESSZIMMER
7. DRIVEWAY ZUFARHTSWEG
8. GARAGE GARAGE
9. HOUSE HAUS
10. KITCHEN KÜCHE
11. LAUNDRY ROOM WASCHKÜCHE
12. LAWN RASEN
13. LIVING ROOM WOHNZIMMER
14. ROOF DACH
15. WINDOW FENSTER

PUZZLE 101

1. BATHTUB BADEWANNE
2. CHANDELIER KRONLEUCHTER
3. CURTAIN VORHANG
4. DRESSER KOMMODE
5. FAUCET WASSERHAHN
6. FENCE ZAUN
7. FIREPLACE KAMIN
8. LIGHT BULB GLÜHLAMPE
9. LOVESEAT ZWEISITZER
10. POOL SCHWIMMBECKEN
11. PORCH VORBAU
12. SOFA SOFA
13. TABLE TISCH
14. WASHER WASCHMASCHINE

PUZZLE 102

1. ARMCHAIR ARMLEHNSTUHL
2. ARMOIRE KLEIDERSCHRANK
3. BIDET BIDET
4. CHIMNEY SCHORNSTEIN
5. CLOSET GARDEROBE
6. CRIB GITTERBETT
7. DESK SCHREIBTISCH
8. HALL DIELE
9. HIGH CHAIR HOCHSTUHL
10. MIRROR SPIEGEL
11. REFRIGERATOR KÜHLSCHRANK
12. SHOWER DUSCHE
13. SINK WASCHBECKEN
14. STAIRS TREPPE

PUZZLE 103

1. TABLESPOON ESSLÖFFEL
2. FORK GABEL
3. GLASS GLAS
4. SPOON LÖFFEL
5. KNIFE MESSER
6. PEPPER SHAKER PFEFFERSTREUER
7. SALAD BOWL SALATSCHÜSSEL
8. SALT SHAKER SALZSTREUER
9. NAPKIN SERVIETTE
10. STEAK KNIFE STEAKMESSER
11. TEAPOT TEEKANNE
12. TEASPOON TEELÖFFEL
13. PLATE TELLER
14. WATER PITCHER WASSERKRUG
15. SUGAR BOWL ZUCKERDOSE

PUZZLE 104

1. BOLTS SCHRAUBEN
2. HAMMER HAMMER
3. LADDER LEITER
4. MALLET HOLZHAMMER
5. NAIL NAGEL
6. NUTS MUTTERN
7. PLIERS ZANGEN
8. SAW SÄGE
9. SCREW SCHRAUBE
10. SCREWDRIVER SCHRAUBENZIEHER
11. TAPE MEASURE MESSBAND
12. WRENCH SCHLÜSSEL

PUZZLE 105

1. BATHROBE BADEMANTEL
2. BELT GÜRTEL
3. DRESS KLEID
4. GLOVES HANDSCHUHE
5. HAT HUT
6. JACKET JACKE
7. NECKTIE KRAWATTE
8. PAJAMAS SCHLAFANZUG
9. PANTS HOSE
10. PANTY HOSE STRUMPFHOSE
11. SHOES SCHUHE
12. SHORTS SHORTS
13. SOCKS SOCKEN
14. STOCKING STRUMPF
15. VEST WESTE

PUZZLE 106

1. BLOUSE BLUSE
2. BOOTS STIEFEL
3. BOW TIE FLIEGE
4. BRIEFS SLIP
5. CLOTHING KLEIDUNG
6. JEANS JEANS
7. RAINCOAT REGENMANTEL
8. SANDALS SANDALEN
9. SHIRT HEMD
10. SKIRT ROCK
11. SUIT ANZUG
12. SUSPENDERS HOSENTRÄGER
13. SWIM SUIT BADEANZUG
14. T-SHIRT T-SHIRT
15. UNDERWEAR UNTERWÄSCHE

PUZZLE 107

1. PENDANT ANHÄNGER
2. BRACELET ARMBAND
3. BROOCH BROSCHE
4. DIAMOND DIAMANT
5. NECKLACE HALSKETTE
6. LOCKET MEDAILLON
7. EARRINGS OHRRINGE
8. OPAL OPAL
9. PEARLS PERLEN
10. RING RING
11. RUBY RUBIN
12. SAPPHIRE SAPHIR
13. EMERALD SMARAGD
14. TOPAZ TOPAS
15. WATCH UHR

PUZZLE 108

1. COMB KAMM
2. CONDITIONER HAARSPÜLUNG
3. CONTACT LENSES KONTAKTLINSEN
4. DENTAL FLOSS ZAHNSEIDE
5. DEODORANT DEODORANT
6. HAIR DRYER FÖN
7. LIPSTICK LIPPENSTIFT
8. MOUTHWASH MUNDWASSER
9. NAIL CLIPPERS NAGELKNIPSER
10. RAZOR RASIERAPPARAT
11. SHAMPOO SHAMPOO
12. TOOTHBRUSH ZAHNBÜRSTE
13. TOOTHPASTE ZAHNPASTA

PUZZLE 109

1. BASEBALL BASEBALL
2. BASKETBALL BASKETBALLSPIEL
3. BOXING BOXEN
4. FENCING FECHTSPORT
5. FIGURE SKATING EISKUNSTLAUF
6. GYMNASTICS GERÄTETURNEN
7. ICE HOCKEY EISHOCKEY
8. SOCCER FUßBALL
9. SWIMMING SCHWIMMEN
10. TENNIS TENNIS
11. VOLLEYBALL VOLLEYBALLSPIEL
12. WRESTLING RINGEN

PUZZLE 110

1. BOBSLED BOBSCHLITTEN
2. CRICKET CRICKET
3. CROSS COUNTRY SKIING SKILANGLAUF
4. DIVING KUNSTSPRINGEN
5. HIGH JUMP HOCHSPRUNG
6. JAVELIN SPEER
7. LONG JUMP WEITSPRUNG
8. LUGE RENNRODEL
9. POLE VAULT STABHOCHSPRUNG
10. SPEED SKATING EISSCHNELLLAUF
11. TABLE TENNIS TISCHTENNIS
12. TRIPLE JUMP DREISPRUNG
13. WATER POLO WASSERBALLSPIEL

PUZZLE 111

1. BAR BAR
2. BRIDGE BRÜCKE
3. OFFICE BÜRO
4. CATHEDRAL DOM
5. AIRPORT FLUGHAFEN
6. CEMETARY FRIEDHOF
7. DEPARTMENT STORE KAUFHAUS
8. MOVIE THEATER KINO
9. HOSPITAL KRANKENHAUS
10. LIGHTHOUSE LEUCHTTURM
11. MUSEUM MUSEUM
12. POST OFFICE POSTAMT
13. SCHOOL SCHULE
14. STADIUM STADION
15. SUPERMARKET SUPERMARKT

PUZZLE 112

1. BANK BANK
2. CASTLE BURG
3. CITY HALL RATHAUS
4. DOWNTOWN INNENSTADT
5. HARBOR HAFEN
6. HOTEL HOTEL
7. LIBRARY BIBLIOTHEK
8. OPERA HOUSE OPERNHAUS
9. PARK PARK
10. PARKING LOT PARKPLATZ
11. PHARMACY APOTHEKE
12. RESTAURANT RESTAURANT
13. STORE GESCHÄFT
14. THEATER THEATER
15. UNIVERSITY UNIVERSITÄT

PUZZLE 113

1. BOOKSTORE BUCHHANDLUNG
2. BOWLING ALLEY BOWLINGBAHN
3. BUS STATION BUSBAHNHOF
4. CHURCH KIRCHE
5. COFFEE SHOP CAFÉ
6. DAM DAMM
7. FIRE STATION FEUERWACHE
8. FLORIST BLUMENLADEN
9. GOLF COURSE GOLFPLATZ
10. MOSQUE MOSCHEE
11. POLICE STATION POLIZEIREVIER
12. RAILROAD STATION BAHNHOF
13. SUBWAY STATION U-BAHN-STATION
14. SYNAGOGUE SYNAGOGE

PUZZLE 114

1. AUTOMOBILE AUTO
2. BUS BUS
3. CAR WAGEN
4. COACH REISEBUS
5. CONVERTIBLE KABRIOLETT
6. MINIVAN MINIBUS
7. MOPED MOFA
8. MOTORCYCLE MOTORRAD
9. PICKUP TRUCK PICKUP
10. SPORTS CAR SPORTWAGEN
11. SUV GELÄNDEWAGEN
12. STATION WAGON KOMBI
13. STREETCAR STRAßENBAHN
14. TRUCK LASTWAGEN

PUZZLE 115

1. BOAT BOOT
2. BICYCLE FAHRRAD
3. AIRPLANE FLUGZEUG
4. HELICOPTER HUBSCHRAUBER
5. CANOE KANU
6. CITY BUS LINIENBUS
7. FIRE TRUCK LÖSCHFAHRZEUG
8. TANK PANZER
9. POLICE CAR POLIZEIFAHRZEUG
10. AMBULANCE RETTUNGSWAGEN
11. SCHOOL BUS SCHULBUS
12. SUBWAY U-BAHN
13. SUBMARINE UNTERSEEBOOT
14. TRAIN ZUG

PUZZLE 116

1. ARABIC ARABISCH
2. ENGLISH ENGLISCH
3. FRENCH FRANZÖSISCH
4. GERMAN DEUTSCH
5. GREEK GRIECHISCH
6. ITALIAN ITALIENISCH
7. JAPANESE JAPANISCH
8. KOREAN KOREANISCH
9. MANDARIN MANDARIN
10. POLISH POLNISCH
11. PORTUGUESE PORTUGIESISCH
12. RUSSIAN RUSSISCH
13. SPANISH SPANISCH
14. THAI THAI

PUZZLE 117

1. BULGARIAN BULGARISCH
2. DUTCH NIEDERLÄNDISCH
3. FINNISH FINNISCH
4. HEBREW HEBRÄISCH
5. HINDI HINDI
6. INDONESIAN INDONESISCH
7. PERSIAN PERSISCH
8. ROMANIAN RUMÄNISCH
9. SWAHILI SUAHELI
10. SWEDISH SCHWEDISCH
11. TURKISH TÜRKISCH
12. URDU URDU
13. VIETNAMESE VIETNAMESISCH

PUZZLE 118

1. ACTOR SCHAUSPIELER
2. ARCHITECT ARCHITEKT
3. CARPENTER ZIMMERMANN
4. CHEF KÜCHENCHEF
5. DENTIST ZAHNARZT
6. DOCTOR ARTZ
7. ELECTRICIAN ELEKTRIKER
8. ENGINEER INGENIEUR
9. LAWYER RECHTSANWALT
10. PILOT PILOT
11. POLICE OFFICER POLIZEIBEAMTER
12. PSYCHIATRIST PSYCHIATER
13. TEACHER LEHRER

PUZZLE 119

1. EARTH ERDE
2. JUPITER JUPITER
3. CRATER KRATER
4. MARS MARS
5. MERCURY MERKUR
6. MOON MOND
7. NEPTUNE NEPTUN
8. PLUTO PLUTO
9. SATURN SATURN
10. SUN SONNE
11. SOLAR SYSTEM SONNENSYSTEM
12. TOTAL ECLIPSE TOTALE FINSTERNIS
13. URANUS URANUS
14. VENUS VENUS
15. FULL MOON VOLLMOND

PUZZLE 120

1. ACCORDION AKKORDEON
2. BAGPIPES DUDELSACK
3. BONGOS BONGOS
4. CELLO CELLO
5. CYMBALS BECKEN
6. DRUMS TROMMELN
7. GUITAR GITARRE
8. HARMONICA MUNDHARMONIKA
9. ORGAN ORGEL
10. PIANO FLÜGEL
11. SAXOPHONE SAXOPHON
12. TAMBOURINE TAMBURIN
13. TRUMPET TROMPETE
14. TUBA TUBA
15. VIOLIN VIOLINE

PUZZLE 121

1. APRICOT APRIKOSE
2. ARCHITECT ARCHITEKT
3. BOBSLED BOBSCHLITTEN
4. BRACELET ARMBAND
5. DOLPHIN DELPHIN
6. FRENCH FRANZÖSISCH
7. GOAT ZIEGE
8. MOPED MOFA
9. PERSIAN PERSISCH
10. POULTRY GEFLÜGEL
11. SUGAR ZUCKER
12. TEA TEE
13. TO BE SEIN
14. UNIVERSITY UNIVERSITÄT
15. YELLOW GELB

PUZZLE 122

1. ASPARAGUS SPARGEL
2. BANK BANK
3. BAT FLEDERMAUS
4. COUSIN VETTER
5. COW KUH
6. EYE AUGE
7. FREEZING RAIN GEFRIERENDER REGEN
8. HALIBUT HEILBUTT
9. LEG BEIN
10. MUSCLES MUSKELN
11. NOSE NASE
12. ONE EIN
13. SATURDAY SAMSTAG
14. WEEKEND WOCHENENDE
15. WOLF WOLF

PUZZLE 123

1. BATHROBE BADEMANTEL
2. BOULEVARD BOULEVARD
3. BLACKBERRIES BROMBEEREN
4. GRANDSON ENKEL
5. DONKEY ESEL
6. FISH FISCH
7. FLAMINGO FLAMINGO
8. BRAIN GEHIRN
9. BELT GÜRTEL
10. HIP HÜFTE
11. TO RUN RENNEN
12. BEDROOM SCHLAFZIMMER
13. SHOES SCHUHE
14. BLACK SCHWARZ
15. SOUTH AMERICA SÜDAMERIKA

PUZZLE 124

1. ALGAE ALGEN
2. ASIA ASIEN
3. BAGPIPES DUDELSACK
4. BLOUSE BLUSE
5. CRIB GITTERBETT
6. CYMBALS BECKEN
7. DAY TAG
8. GLOVES HANDSCHUHE
9. ISLAND INSEL
10. MUSEUM MUSEUM
11. OCTAGON ACHTECK
12. ORANGUTAN ORANG-UTAN
13. POOL SCHWIMMBECKEN
14. SEPTEMBER SEPTEMBER
15. SHOULDER SCHULTER

PUZZLE 125

1. AUNT TANTE
2. AUTOMOBILE AUTO
3. CHIPMUNK BACKENHÖRNCHEN
4. DRUMS TROMMELN
5. FAUCET WASSERHAHN
6. HAND HAND
7. HELICOPTER HUBSCHRAUBER
8. HUMMINGBIRD KOLIBRI
9. MONUMENT DENKMAL
10. NEPTUNE NEPTUN
11. PRIMATES PRIMATEN
12. SEA MEER
13. SUBWAY U-BAHN
14. SYNAGOGUE SYNAGOGE
15. YEAR JAHR

PUZZLE 126

1. DUCK ENTE
2. FAMILY FAMILIE
3. FULL MOON VOLLMOND
4. HEBREW HEBRÄISCH
5. ITALIAN ITALIENISCH
6. LIBRARY BIBLIOTHEK
7. LOBSTER HUMMER
8. MONDAY MONTAG
9. OCTOPUS TINTENFISCH
10. RED ROT
11. TEN ZEHN
12. TO DO TUN
13. TO WORK ARBEITEN
14. TWENTY ZWANZIG
15. WRESTLING RINGEN

PUZZLE 127

1. COFFEE SHOP CAFÉ
2. SMALL INTESTINE DÜNNDARM
3. PALM HANDFLÄCHE
4. HURRICANE HURRIKAN
5. STATION WAGON KOMBI
6. HEAD KOPF
7. IGUANA LEGUAN
8. BABOON PAVIAN
9. ROSEMARY ROSMARIN
10. JUICE SAFT
11. BOLTS SCHRAUBEN
12. TO SEE SEHEN
13. SEVEN SIEBEN
14. SON SOHN
15. SUMMER SOMMER

PUZZLE 128

1. ANISE ANIS
2. AUTUMN HERBST
3. CARIBOU RENTIER
4. EIGHTEEN ACHTZEHN
5. JAGUAR JAGUAR
6. PROVINCE PROVINZ
7. SEA LION SEELÖWE
8. TABLE TISCH
9. TEETH ZÄHNE
10. THREE DREI
11. TO LEAVE ABFAHREN
12. TO PLAY SPIELEN
13. TRIPLE JUMP DREISPRUNG
14. TYPHOON TAIFUN
15. VEINS VENEN

PUZZLE 129

1. AFRICA AFRIKA
2. AVENUE ALLEE
3. CHAMELEON CHAMÄLEON
4. GARLIC KNOBLAUCH
5. LETTUCE SALAT
6. MEDITERRANEAN SEA MITTELMEER
7. PELICAN PELIKAN
8. PLIERS ZANGEN
9. SHEEP SCHAF
10. SHOULDER BLADE SCHULTERBLATT
11. SOFA SOFA
12. SQUIRREL EICHHÖRNCHEN
13. WINDOW FENSTER
14. WOODPECKER SPECHT
15. YEAR JAHR

PUZZLE 130

1. BALCONY BALKON
2. BULGARIAN BULGARISCH
3. COUGAR PUMA
4. CREAM SAHNE
5. CYAN ZYAN
6. EGGS EIER
7. EVENING ABEND
8. MONTH MONAT
9. ONE HUNDRED HUNDERT
10. PLUMS PFLAUMEN
11. STREET STRAßE
12. TEMPLE SCHLÄFE
13. THIGH OBERSCHENKEL
14. YELLOW PEPPER GELBER PAPRIKA
15. WATERMELON WASSERMELONE

PUZZLE 131

1. ELEVEN ELF
2. GOOSE GANS
3. GREEN BEAN GRÜNE BOHNE
4. SKIN HAUT
5. SUSPENDERS HOSENTRÄGER
6. CHEF KÜCHENCHEF
7. RECTUM MASTDARM
8. MOTORCYCLE MOTORRAD
9. EARRINGS OHRRINGE
10. PARSNIP PASTINAKE
11. POLISH POLNISCH
12. SALT SALZ
13. STREETCAR STRAßENBAHN
14. THOUSAND TAUSEND
15. TO UNDERSTAND VERSTEHEN

PUZZLE 132

1. FENNEL FENCHEL
2. FLORIST BLUMENLADEN
3. FORTY VIERZIG
4. LADYBUG MARIENKÄFER
5. PLATE TELLER
6. PORPOISE TÜMMLER
7. SALAMANDER SALAMANDER
8. SPRING FRÜHLING
9. STAIRS TREPPE
10. STORE GESCHÄFT
11. SWIM SUIT BADEANZUG
12. TERMITE TERMITE
13. TO DRINK TRINKEN
14. TO WALK GEHEN
15. WHITE WEIß

PUZZLE 133

1. BOWLING ALLEY — BOWLINGBAHN
2. CROCODILE — KROKODIL
3. GORILLA — GORILLA
4. GUITAR — GITARRE
5. HEDGEHOG — IGEL
6. HOSPITAL — KRANKENHAUS
7. HOTEL — HOTEL
8. HOUSE — HAUS
9. MINUTE — MINUTE
10. PLUTO — PLUTO
11. PUMPKIN — KÜRBIS
12. SEVENTEEN — SIEBZEHN
13. SQUID — KALMAR
14. TEASPOON — TEELÖFFEL
15. VEGETABLES — GEMÜSE

PUZZLE 134

1. GREEN — GRÜN
2. HONEYBEE — HONIGBIENE
3. JUNE — JUNI
4. KNEE — KNIE
5. KOREAN — KOREANISCH
6. MAY — MAI
7. POLICE STATION — POLIZEIREVIER
8. PORTUGUESE — PORTUGIESISCH
9. RACCOON — WASCHBÄR
10. SKIRT — ROCK
11. SKUNK — STINKTIER
12. SOUR CREAM — SAURE SAHNE
13. TO BUY — KAUFEN
14. TO LOVE — LIEBEN
15. TO TAKE — NEHMEN

PUZZLE 135

1. BONGOS — BONGOS
2. PENTAGON — FÜNFECK
3. FIFTY — FÜNFZIG
4. DOG — HUND
5. DOWNTOWN — INNENSTADT
6. CHIN — KINN
7. RED PEPPER — ROTER PAPRIKA
8. SALAD BOWL — SALATSCHÜSSEL
9. TO CLOSE — SCHLIEßEN
10. STARFISH — SEESTERN
11. SEVENTY — SIEBZIG
12. FOUR — VIER
13. SUBURBS — VORORTE
14. WEEK — WOCHE
15. TWELVE — ZWÖLF

PUZZLE 136

1. AIRPLANE — FLUGZEUG
2. BASKETBALL — BASKETBALLSPIEL
3. BROWN — BRAUN
4. COMB — KAMM
5. FRIDAY — FREITAG
6. GRANDDAUGHTER — ENKELIN
7. GUINEA PIG — MEERSCHWEINCHEN
8. OSTRICH — STRAUß
9. PENDANT — ANHÄNGER
10. RASPBERRIES — HIMBEEREN
11. SAGE — SALBEI
12. SHARK — HAI
13. TO BE ABLE TO — KÖNNEN
14. TO CARRY — TRAGEN
15. VIOLIN — VIOLINE

PUZZLE 137

1. BREAD — BROT
2. CHURCH — KIRCHE
3. CORIANDER — KORIANDER
4. DRESS — KLEID
5. DRESSER — KOMMODE
6. DUCK — ENTE
7. FOURTEEN — VIERZEHN
8. HINDI — HINDI
9. PAJAMAS — SCHLAFANZUG
10. POLAR BEAR — EISBÄR
11. SAPPHIRE — SAPHIR
12. SAVORY — BOHNENKRAUT
13. SCHOOL — SCHULE
14. TO ASK — FRAGEN
15. TONGUE — ZUNGE

PUZZLE 138

1. ATLANTIC OCEAN — ATLANTIK
2. CELLO — CELLO
3. DINING ROOM — ESSZIMMER
4. FINNISH — FINNISCH
5. HIGH JUMP — HOCHSPRUNG
6. HYENA — HYÄNE
7. LARGE INTESTINE — DICKDARM
8. MILK — MILCH
9. NAIL CLIPPERS — NAGELKNIPSER
10. NOVEMBER — NOVEMBER
11. OPAL — OPAL
12. RADISH — RADIESCHEN
13. SIXTY — SECHZIG
14. TODAY — HEUTE
15. TOTAL ECLIPSE — TOTALE FINSTERNIS

PUZZLE 139

1. ARTERIES — ARTERIEN
2. THIRTY — DREIßIG
3. FINGER — FINGER
4. SOCCER — FUßBALL
5. GRANDMOTHER — GROßMUTTER
6. NECK — HALS
7. HEART — HERZ
8. HONEY — HONIG
9. RABBIT — KANINCHEN
10. CAT — KATZE
11. OCEANIA — OZEANIEN
12. POLICE OFFICER — POLIZEIBEAMTER
13. BACK — RÜCKEN
14. SISTER-IN-LAW — SCHWÄGERIN
15. DRIZZLE — SPRÜHREGEN

PUZZLE 140

1. BLUE — BLAU
2. BOXING — BOXEN
3. EAR — OHR
4. JACKET — JACKE
5. MONITOR LIZARD — WARAN
6. MOUTHWASH — MUNDWASSER
7. OPOSSUM — OPOSSUM
8. PARENTS — ELTERN
9. REFRIGERATOR — KÜHLSCHRANK
10. RIVER — FLUß
11. SWEDISH — SCHWEDISCH
12. THUNDERSTORM — GEWITTER
13. TIGER — TIGER
14. VOLLEYBALL — VOLLEYBALLSPIEL
15. WHALE — WAL

PUZZLE 141

1. BASEMENT KELLER
2. BELUGA WEIßWAL
3. BUMBLEBEE HUMMEL
4. CEMETARY FRIEDHOF
5. CRICKET CRICKET
6. HARMONICA MUNDHARMONIKA
7. ICE HOCKEY EISHOCKEY
8. LION LÖWE
9. MARS MARS
10. PINEAPPLE ANANAS
11. SUIT ANZUG
12. SUNDAY SONNTAG
13. TO HELP HELFEN
14. TO WRITE SCHREIBEN
15. WEDNESDAY MITTWOCH

PUZZLE 142

1. BISON BISON
2. BRIEFS SLIP
3. CAR WAGEN
4. CRAB KRABBE
5. DRAGONFLY LIBELLE
6. FATHER VATER
7. GARAGE GARAGE
8. GLASS GLAS
9. MEAT FLEISCH
10. MOSQUITO MOSKITO
11. STATE BUNDESSTAAT
12. TO DANCE TANZEN
13. TO READ LESEN
14. TRUMPET TROMPETE
15. WATER POLO WASSERBALLSPIEL

PUZZLE 143

1. TO CHANGE ÄNDERN
2. ANTELOPE ANTILOPE
3. THIRTEEN DREIZEHN
4. FEBRUARY FEBRUAR
5. FISH FISCH
6. JULY JULI
7. CHANDELIER KRONLEUCHTER
8. KITCHEN KÜCHE
9. SWISS CHARD MANGOLD
10. PENGUIN PINGUIN
11. SPINACH SPINAT
12. PIGEON TAUBE
13. TENNIS TENNIS
14. TUBA TUBA
15. LAUNDRY ROOM WASCHKÜCHE

PUZZLE 144

1. BUS STATION BUSBAHNHOF
2. CAMEL KAMEL
3. DAY TAG
4. EIGHT ACHT
5. HAT HUT
6. HEAVY RAIN STARKER REGEN
7. JANUARY JANUAR
8. LOCKET MEDAILLON
9. PACIFIC OCEAN PAZIFIK
10. PEACH PFIRSICH
11. PICKUP TRUCK PICKUP
12. PLATEAU PLATEAU
13. REPTILES REPTILIEN
14. TURKISH TÜRKISCH
15. WIFE FRAU

PUZZLE 145

1. AIRPORT FLUGHAFEN
2. BIRDS VÖGEL
3. COURTHOUSE VÖGEL
4. ELBOW ELLBOGEN
5. FRUIT FRÜCHTE
6. HUSBAND EHEMANN
7. MOON MOND
8. OIL ÖL
9. PILOT PILOT
10. PORCUPINE STACHELSCHWEIN
11. STOCKING STRUMPF
12. TEACHER LEHRER
13. TWO ZWEI
14. WINTER WINTER
15. WRIST HANDGELENK

PUZZLE 146

1. HAMSTER HAMSTER
2. KNIFE MESSER
3. LUGE RENNRODEL
4. MAMMALS SÄUGETIERE
5. MOSQUE MOSCHEE
6. NAPKIN SERVIETTE
7. NARWHAL NARWAL
8. NIECE NICHTE
9. PARK PARK
10. PINK ROSA
11. SIX SECHS
12. TO SELL VERKAUFEN
13. TROPICAL STORM TROPISCHER STURM
14. TURKEY TRUTHAHN
15. UNCLE ONKEL

PUZZLE 147

1. EAGLE ADLER
2. BATHTUB BADEWANNE
3. ROOF DACH
4. CATHEDRAL DOM
5. TO GO GEHEN
6. BUTTOCK GESÄß
7. MALLET HOLZHAMMER
8. TAPE MEASURE MESSBAND
9. POLICE CAR POLIZEIFAHRZEUG
10. LAKE SEE
11. MIRROR SPIEGEL
12. TO LOOK FOR SUCHEN
13. DAUGHTER TOCHTER
14. WASHER WASCHMASCHINE
15. CICADA ZIKADE

PUZZLE 148

1. ALLIGATOR ALLIGATOR
2. ARM ARM
3. CASTLE BURG
4. DENTAL FLOSS ZAHNSEIDE
5. KILLER WHALE SCHWERTWAL
6. LIVING ROOM WOHNZIMMER
7. ONION ZWIEBEL
8. ORANGE ORANGE
9. PIG SCHWEIN
10. PORCH VORBAU
11. STRAWBERRIES ERDBEEREN
12. TO COOK KOCHEN
13. TUESDAY DIENSTAG
14. VIPER VIPER
15. ZUCCHINI ZUCCHINI

PUZZLE 149

1. AFTERNOON NACHMITTAG
2. ARACHNIDS SPINNENTIERE
3. CHEETAH GEPARD
4. FLEA FLOH
5. GOOSE GANS
6. MERCURY MERKUR
7. MOVIE THEATER KINO
8. SATURN SATURN
9. SOCKS SOCKEN
10. TARRAGON ESTRAGON
11. TO OWE SCHULDEN
12. TO WANT WOLLEN
13. TOE ZEH
14. VULTURE GEIER
15. WALLABY WALLABY

PUZZLE 150

1. AMBULANCE RETTUNGSWAGEN
2. BAR BAR
3. BOAT BOOT
4. HAIL HAGEL
5. LIZARD EIDECHSE
6. MARGARINE MARGARINE
7. NINE NEUN
8. PARSLEY PETERSILIE
9. SALT SHAKER SALZSTREUER
10. TABLE TENNIS TISCHTENNIS
11. TEMPERATURE TEMPERATUR
12. TO HAVE HABEN
13. UNDERWEAR UNTERWÄSCHE
14. VEST WESTE
15. VIOLET VIOLETT

Congratulations

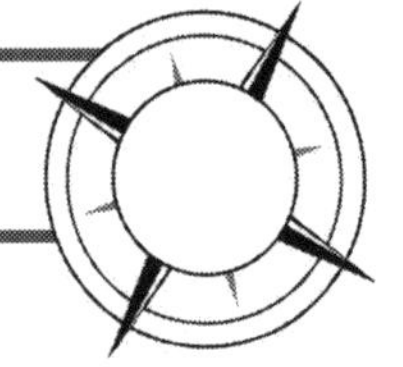

You have now completed
Learn German with Wordsearch Puzzles.

If you enjoyed this book, please feel free to check out our other language learning Wordsearch puzzle books!

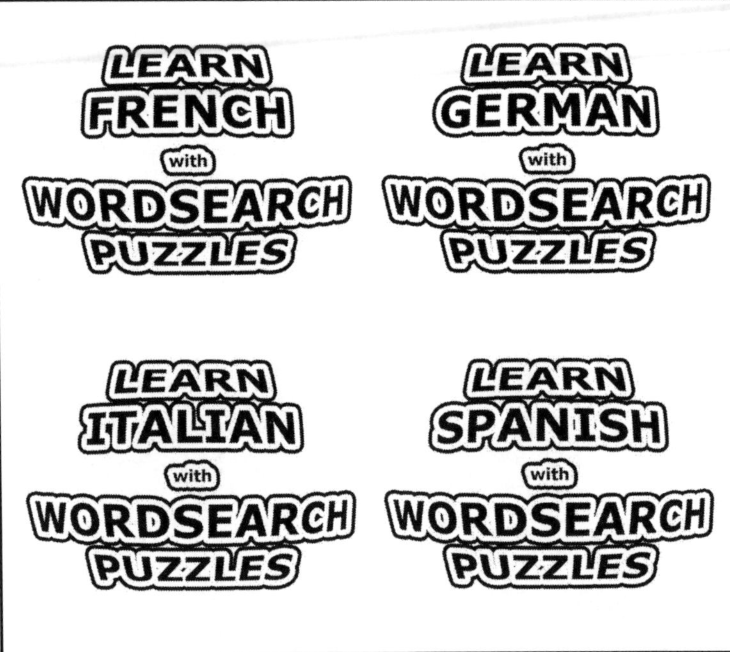

Made in the USA
Monee, IL
01 November 2019

16203364R00098